# Moradi Medical Biochemistry

Mehran Moradi

Pouyan Asadi

Peyman Hadi

Elahe Alivaisi

Saeed Parshang

Mehdi Khorshid Talab

Shbnam Varzeshi

Title: Moradi Medical Biochemistry

Edited by: Mehran Moradi

Authors: Mehran Moradi, Pouyan Asadi, Peyman Hadi, Elahe Alivaisi, Saeed Parshang, Mehdi Khorshid Talab, Shbnam Varzeshi,

ISBN: 9781939123350

Publisher: Supreme Century, USA

Prepare for Publishing: Asan Nashr

© Mehran Moradi

All Rights Reserved

# Table of Contents

Foreword ..................................................................................8

Chapter1 ..................................................................................9

   Urine of biochemistry ............................................................9

   Action of kidney in the body ..................................................9

   The clinical significance of urine analysis: ...........................10

   Types of urine samples: .......................................................12

   Transport and storage of urine samples: .............................13

   Preservative: ........................................................................15

   Urine analysis: .....................................................................17

   Urine color or color of urine ................................................19

   Different appearance of urine ..............................................22

   Specific gravity: ...................................................................24

   Foam: ...................................................................................27

   Urine chemical reagents: .....................................................28

   Glucose measurement or measurement of glucose in urine: ...29

   Galactosuria: ........................................................................30

   fluroglosinol test: .................................................................30

   Confirmatory test: ................................................................31

   Causes an increase and decrease urobilinogen: ..................32

   Ketonuria: ............................................................................33

   PH: .......................................................................................34

   Dual detector system: ..........................................................34

   Blood in urine: .....................................................................36

   Renal proteinuria: ................................................................39

- Nitrite in urine: ................................................................................ 41
- RBC in urine: .................................................................................. 44
- WBC in urine .................................................................................. 48
- Epithelial cells ................................................................................ 50
- Urinary crystals .............................................................................. 54
- Urinary casts: ................................................................................. 58

Chapter2 ............................................................................................. 71
- Water and electrolytes .................................................................. 71
- Solubility ........................................................................................ 72
- Osmosis .......................................................................................... 73
- Homeostasis ................................................................................... 74
- Sodium reduction ........................................................................... 75
- PH measurement equations ........................................................... 81
- Hypoxia .......................................................................................... 94
- Metabolic acidosis .......................................................................... 95
- Respiratory acidosis ....................................................................... 98
- Metabolic alkalosis ......................................................................... 99
- Respiratory alkalosis .................................................................... 101
- Electrolytes and minerals: ............................................................ 104

Chapter 3 ........................................................................................... 115
- Digestion and absorption of carbohydrates in the body ............. 116
- Metabolic Disruption : .................................................................. 129
- GlucosilarHomoglobin(HbA1c): .................................................... 131
- Diabetes Distinction Standards .................................................... 131

- ❖ Oftalmoplegia: By shedding light into the eye pupil with no reaction. 152
- ❖ ataxia: wobble (like taking alcohol), have difficulty In the speaking. 152
- ❖ encephalopathy(alcoholinterfereswith theabsorption of vitaminB1). 152
- ❖ .................................................................................................. 152
- ❖ anti-seizure drugs, such as barbiturates (anti-seizure) is applicable In the this case. ................................................................................ 152
- ❖ neuritis: inflammation neuronal ....................................................... 152
- ❖ thiamine deficiency affects on the peripheral nervous system and the heart. ................................................................................................ 152
- ❖ thiamine deficiencysymptoms: mentaldisturbance, ataxia, and Oftalmoplegia. ................................................................................... 152

**How can Discerned if a person is vitamin deficiency B1 or not?** ......... 152

Chapter4 ............................................................................................. 214

    Liver ............................................................................................ 214

Chapter 5 ............................................................................................ 224

    Plasma lipids .............................................................................. 224

Refrences ............................................................................................ 241

# Foreword

Biochemical medicine is a collection of knowledge and different skills like chemistry ، biochemistry، physiology and other related sciences that uses to diagnose the disease and first of all, it searches essential information related to the value and ability of experimental tests in diagnosing and then effect of disease cure by using special methods and without any order and classification, everybody confused.

Sorting subjects in biochemical medicine causes scientific cure that becomes certainly the turning-point of science transformation. One of reasons that causes we compile this book, is drawing students attention relative to new point-view in better comprehension from biochemical medicine that causes better comprehension in complex biochemical procedures.

We hope the dear teahers and students could use this book.

**Mehran Moradi**

# Chapter1

## Urine of biochemistry

70 percent of experiments are biochemical experiment. urine was first specimen that examined in laboratory. In the past , urologist analyzed the urine and didn't visit the patients but examined the urine. Volume, color, scent, viscosity were examined to identify disease and tasting the specimen were current.

There were a chart to analyze the urine in the middle ages. The urine comes from kidney. Cortex and medulla constitute the kidney. Nephron is the smallest part of kidney. an artery brings the blood to the nephron and another artery exits from glumerol.

## Action of kidney in the body

1. Excretion of material that include: products of protein catabolism (urea, creatinine, uric acid) organic and inorganic acids, bases also harmful substrates, toxic and drugs comes in our body.

2. Regulation of fluid, electrolyte and acid-base balance of blood

3. Endocrine function of kidney that including or include: rennin hormone synthesis, erythropoietin, prostaglandins, also activation of vitamin D and some other hormones

## The clinical significance of urine analysis:

1. Checking the status of the kidney and urinary tract by Appearance, blood, protein, nitrite, leukocyte esterase, urinary sediment

2. metabolic disease survey:

ph, appearance, sugar, ketones, bilirubin, orbilinogen

3. systemic disease survey:

can diagnosed hemoglobin, myoblogin, porfilinogen, light chain protein of immunoglobin, renal and prostate cancer by urine or can diagnose by urine

Urine production:

Approximately 25% of cardiac output enters the kidney

In normal adults 12000ml/min blood enter in to kidney

Glumerol filters 170-200 litre liquid that reabsorbed in passing from tubes and reaches the urine volume to 600-2000ml in 24 hours.

Any disruption in kidney function lead to systemic or kidney disease is reflected in urine by chemical or cytology changes

Urine collected from urine:

Method of sampling→ feasible test

1. routine void → routine test of urine or urine routine test
2. midstream clean catch→ urine culture cytology
3. catheter(urinary tract)→urine routine test- urine culture
4. Catheter(urethral)→ the distinctions between a bladder and kidney infection
5. superabubic→ urine routine test- urine culture test
6. urine collection bag→ urine routine test, quantification measurements or measurement of quantification

Table 1: ways to sample from urine

To culture the urine, examin the middle urine.

Suprapubic; catheter connected to a patient and sample are taken directly from the bladder

## Types of urine samples:

| Type of sample | application | Limitation and error |
|---|---|---|
| random | Suitable for cytology test | Doesn't show patients condition exactly, if consume liquid and sport |
| morning | The most concentrated sample for routine test and proteinuria | unsuitable for cytology test |
| several time | Studied of diabetes whit GTT samples | Water deprivation test |
| timer | Quantitative measurement, clearance calculate | cytology |

Table2: types of urine sample

The athletes since proteins and other cells exit, the blood enters in the urine.

For water deprivation test, because we want to check the power of kidney, we sample periodically.

## Transport and storage of urine samples:

In instances where remaining more than two hours or container should be used container

There aren't any containers that suitable for all of the experiment

Cell and material damage in alkaline urine can be done faster

In ph acidity and specific gravity more than 1/015 cell deterioration occurs later

Due to acidosis respiratory that occur during the sleep, early morning urine has less PH.

A scientist named who said, use a preserver for long-term preserving, preserver affect on urine tests and changes experiments answer.

Alkaline ph, rbc in urine are destroyed

When sleep, apnea can cause acidosis respiratory

Physical change in unprotected samples:

Color:to be reduced and oxidized of materials, causes:

Conversion of biliverdin to bilirubin

Conversion of urobilin to urobilinogen

Conversion of met hemoglobin to hemoglobin

Odor (decomposition of urine to ammonia by bacteria in the urine)

Psudoincrease is due to pseudomonas bacteria growth

Transparence: false reduce visibility due to bacteria growth causing precipitation of dissolve material (crystals and amorphous material)

| | |
|---|---|
| Increase decomposition of urea to ammonia by urease-positive bacteria<br>Increase co₂ lose<br>Decrease glucose conversion to acids by bacteria and yests | ph |
| Increase of glycolyses by cells and urine bacteria | glucose |
| Reduce conversion of acetone to acetoacetate and evaporation of acetone | ketone |
| Decrease of bilirubin photooxidation and converts to biliverdin | bilirobine |
| Decrease of photo oxidation and conversion to bilirobine | urobilinogen |
| Increase of bacteria growth in the remaining sample | nitrite |

Table3: chemical change in unprotected sample

Cellular changes in unprotected sample:

Cell: reduce of degradation and demolition occurred in dilute and alkaline samples

Cylinder: the degradation occurred in dilute an alkaline samples, cylinder are solved in alkaline urine

Bacteria: increase of growth and reproduction of bacteria occurs.

## Preservative:
1. Samples were kept in refrigerator: or preservative of sample in

In routine test if testing done about two hours, the refrigerator is not recommend

To inhibit bacteria growth, keep samples in refrigerator over two hours

Such as or an sample can be used for cultivation

Refrigerator deposit is urate amorphous an phosphate

If there are sediment in the urine because of coldness or there are some crystals in it, first we should put it in ben mary in 37c (equal to the body) and then examine.

2. Freezing:

Suitable method for measuring bilirubin, urobilinogen and some hormones

Freezing are causing loss of element in urine

3. Formalin 40% (a drop for 10 ml)

Protection from the elements in urine

Excessive use of formaldehyde cause protein precipitation, the second, third and fourth structure of protein have or had weak ties, so destroys these weak bonds and denatures the protein sediment.

4. Boric acid whit concentration 1gr/dl:

Protection of protein, material and cells that presence in urine precipitation

Boric acid to stop the bacteria growth over 24 hours

In routine test just have interface whit ph

It causes amorph urate precipitation.

Each crystal is making in acidic ph, in due to uses of boric acid have been misdiagnosed

5. thymol (multi-pieces crystals)

Protect of elements in the urine

Prevent growth of bacteria and yeasts

Thymol interference whit protein precipitation experiment

6. Hydrochloric acid 2-normalized

Bactericide and destroys sediment elements

This material is unsuitable for routine test, urine cultures and the solution will precipitate.

This substance is very useful for gathering 24 hours urine to quantitive measurement.

7. saccomannos fixative

Ideal protective for cellular elements in serological test

8. Preservative tablets (a 95mg tablet per 20ml urine)

This material to increase the specific gravity

Release the formaldehyde but no to the extent that changes the reducers to positive

By using these tablets it enables todiagnose the sugar and metabolic diseases.

## Urine analysis:
1. Physical properties
2. Chemical properties
3. Microscopic characteristic

| Microscopic characteristic | Chemical properties |
|---|---|
| 1. wbc | 1. PH |
| 2. RBC | 2. protein |
| 3. EPC | 3. sugar |
| 4. cast | 4. ketone bodies |
| 5. crystal | 5. blood |
| 6. bacteria | 6. nitrite |
| 7. yeast | 7. leukocyte esterase |
| 8. parasite | 8. bilirobine |
| 9. sperm | 9. urobilinogen |
| 10. mucus | 10. Ascorbic acid |

Table4: chemical and microscopic properties of urine analysis

Urine microscopic test or experiments

Color- specific gravity- appearance- odor

Volume

Normal amount of urine product or produce:

1. Adult 1cc at an hour per kg of body weight

2. Children 4cc at an hour per kilogram of body weight

Volumetric abnoramalities:

Normal urine volume 600-200cc: normal amount of urine not be excrete → anuria

Excreted less than 600cc → oliguria

Excreted more than 2000cc → polyuria

**Urine color or color of urine:**

normal urine is yellow

Urokrome: product of body metabolism and there is or presence in plasma, eventually excreted on (in) the urine, urokrome is fat- soluble

Failure chronic renal disease reduced urinary excretion of this substance and finally causes urokrome sediment in lipid of under skin and totally skin becomes yellow.

Urine color change or change of urine color:

Specific disease, an abnormal metabolic, eating or specific drug

Contamination whit non-urinary source

Contamination whit the stool, hemorrhoids and menstrual blood

Effect of light: it is best stored in the dark place until time of specimen experiment.

| Color | cause |
|---|---|
| colorless | Dilute urine by polyuria and consuming liquid |
| Light yellow | Dilute urine |
| Yellow | Norm al urine |
| Amber | Strong urine, orobiline, dehydration, fever |
| Dark amber | Bilirobin, biliverdine |
| Orange | Bilirobin, biliverdine, drugs |
| Red | RBC, hemoglobin, myoglobine, beet, food colors |
| pink | Hemoglobin, porphyrin |
| brown | Methemoglobin, hemogentric acid, melanin, myoglobin |
| black | Melanin, hemogentric acid |
| green | Infection of the small intestine, pseudomonas infection, drugs, color |

Table5: urine color and its reason

Hemogantisic acid: it created from phenylalanine metabolism that darkens the urine nearby the air. hemogantisic acid created in alkaptunory disease too

contamination with non-urinary infection such as: those drugs can use for photography.

bilirobin→ biliverdin (green)

Urine appearance or view: normal urine completely clear

Suspended solids or material involved in urine turbidity

The old sample and were not kept well, bacteria growth that will be cause a dull or cloudy status phosphate and amorphous urate may causes urine turbidity

Clottation is a RBC signature

Milky appearance of urine may be the result of lymph or foam

A clear urine is not essentially a normal urine

Abnormal amount of glucose or protein or even WBC may exist in the urine

## Different appearance of urine

| appearance | status |
|---|---|
| clear | There isn't or there are no visible particle |
| Slightly cloudy | Particles are seen in the sample, the text read at behind of tube |
| cloudy | many particles in the sample, the text read at behind of tube ,but it isn't clear |
| turbid | The transcript text at the behind of the tube isn't visible |

Table 6: different appearance of urine

Between S.C, Clear there is status that named hazy that a scientist named who expressed it but it doesn't report nowhere.

Haze causing substance in the urine:

Pathological:

1) RBC    2) WBC    3) Renal epithelial cell
4) fat (lipid and shilomicron)    5) abnormal crystal    6) bacteria(in fresh urine)    7) yeast, trichomonas    8) rock
9) pus

Non-pathological (their existence do not important in the urine) :

1) Natural crystal of urate and phosphate   2) radiological material

3) Mucus, mosin and worms   4) squamous epithelial

5) Semen   6) pollution

7) leucine   8) powders and talc

Odor:

The guidance of discovery phenylketonuria disease in the past

Report of the urine odor isn't a routine test, because it is not available in organic and inorganic compounds

Unless odor of sample is sever

Old urine be or will determine by sever ammonia odor

If a fresh urine gives a smell ammonia odor, it may indicate a serious infection of the urinary tract

In metabolic disease odor is important because presence of organic and inorganic makes or creates this odor that including:

1: acidosis

2: metabolic disease → ammonium increases in the urine and the urine gives a smell.

3: problem with amonia, valine, luesine, isoluesine cycle → maple syrup disease

Overall maple syrup disease, the type of disease that body doesn't have ability to use of three essential amino acids (valine, leucine, isoleucine). These amino acids are branched.

Individual genetically in $CO_2$ metabolic that is one of thebranched amino acids , as a result of damage to brain cell By Fe-Cl can measure 3 left amino acids in blood and prevents to disease prevelance by diet related to 3 amino acids above.

| odor | cause |
|---|---|
| ammonia | Remain urine |
| Rattlin,stinking | Urine infection |
| Sweet fruit | Starvation, malnutrition, hard exercise, diabetes |
| mouse | phenylketonuria |
| straw | aminoaciduria |
| Maple syrup | Maple syrup disease |
| foxy | Tyrosinemia |
| Spoiled fish | Trimethyl aminori |
| Hale,hops | Methionine malabsorption |

Table7: factors that cause odor in urine

## Specific gravity:

Specific gravity has no units

The weight of a certain volume of urine as compred with weight of the same volume of distilled water at constant temperature are or is called the specific gravity

The concentration of dissolved substances is represent

Random SG of urine are or is variable between 1/035-1/005

Urine specific gravity in 24 hours 1.015-1/022

Maximum SG of urine that excreted from kidney is 1.040

SG of initial ultrafilter luminal space of kidney is 1/010 that changes by passing tubules.

Special gravity shows power of thicking kidney

The specific gravity (24 hours) is important

In normal states doesn't have sg 1/040. Urine of filter to bohman capsule is 1.010 when passing different places, absorbing the substances and SG goes up or down.

Isosthenuria:

State of the specific gravity that can remain at 1.010 limitation

Lack of renal tubules efficient

Usually such as people have or had enuresis

Hyposthenuria

Hypersthenuria

For example; if excreted glucose 50mg it multiplied in four, the result that is 200 subtracted from SG

Sugar and protein, falsely cg are increase

For every 1gr/dl protein, 3 units of SG are or to be low

For every 1gr/dl sugar, 4 units of SG to be or are low

X-ray contrast agents, mannitole, and dextran the false increase of SG ( greaten than 1/050) is causing

Specific gravity greaten than 1/035, is caused by dehydration, proteinuria, glucosuria and lipid necrosis

Low SG, seen in the collagen disease, hypertension, insipid diabetes and the high intake of fluid or liquid or alcohol

Specific gravity and urine volume have inverse relationship whit together

Except some cases such as diabetes mellitus and renal failure

Sometimes instead of water, tea given to the person, why?

Measurement of SG by some methods:

Falling drops (half automatic methods), urinmeter (require large volume of urine)

Urine stripe and refractometer

Refractometer common method that used to measurement of SG

Refraction by solution, the basis of SG measurement by refractometer

This method requires the small amount of urine

It Is carried out in the temperature rang 15-37 of laboratories and doesn't need any temperature correction

To control the device, we can use 5gr/dl NaCl that creates SG in 1+_1.022 limitation or 9gr/dl sacharose that creates SG in 1+_1.034 limitation

To reset the device is used to distilled

There are two types of diabetes insipid:

Central: lack of ADH secretion from the kidneys

Renal: hormone is secreted but any apoporines don't exist to influenced by hormones.

Lipid necrosis: lipid accumulates in upper tract renal epithelial

Their function are destroyed, cell was eliminate and repulsed and the place of the cell will not filled (fibrous filled by connective tissue and replaced )

Damage of kidney, cornea and peripheral nerves exist in diabet.

Following proteinuria had need to lipiduria

A drop of urine for refratometer is enough but large volume are required for urinometer but these are more useful

Protein of serum and plasma can be measured by refractometer


Foam:
Not reported routinely

Normal urine by shaking makes a foam that after while disappears

Moderate to large amount protein of urine (albumin) makes or created or creates white stable foam; in bilirubine whit high amount, obtained yellow foam

Urine chemical test or chemical test of urine:

Based on type of the test the result can be expressed by following form:

- The concentration
- The low- medium- high
- Positive 1- 4
- The normal, negative, positive
- PH , SG whit their unit and expressed by numerical

## Urine chemical reagents:
the most important reason for the use of chemical reagent

- Proven the results previously obtained by stripe
- Test repetition in the urine sample that has strong color
- Reagent more sensitive than stripe
- More feature than strip

Sulfa salicylic acid is used to evaluation of protein

Preparation of reagents must be fit to consumption

Chemical test carried out to confirm strip answer . if the sample has a strong color, we shouldn't use strip.

Glucose in urine (glucosuria):

Normally glucose in urine not seen

Renal threshold for glucose reabsorption is 160-180mg/dl

Prerenal glucosuria: hyperglycemia (diabetes, hormone diseases)

Renal glucosuria: tubular reabsorption defect (pregnant, toxic whit heavy metal)

## Glucose measurement or measurement of glucose in urine:

glucose oxidase method

- If glucose level less than 20mg/dl, it is reported as a negative or normal
- The lower temperature and the higher urine SG, sensitivity of test is lower
- Glucose oxidize method for measuring glucose of urine, if samples of ascorbic acid are more than 50mg/dl, lead to regeneration hydrogen proxide and can be cause false negative result

Glucose oxidize which enzyme that glucose of urine is determinate. Hydrogen peroxide combined whit protein and makes color. Hydrogen peroxide is an oxidizing agent.

Reduced substances (such as vitamin c or ascorbic acid) by elimination OF $H_2O_2$

Spoil the reaction

study of glucose should be simultaneously ascorbic acid is check

### Galactosuria:

check urine for reducing substances

Galactosemia whish disease whit increase of blood galactose (breath fed children) due to an enzyme deficiency led to harsh consequences, such as retardation, thus children under two should be checked for reluctant

### fluroglosinol test:

- associated to bilirobin and urobilinogen complex
- This complex was large and couldn't cross the glomerular barrier
- This mixture going to liver where it is conjugates whit glucoronate
- For any reason conjugated bilirubin get out from the liver and enter the blood, secretsin blood rapidly
- Bilirubin in blood bound to albumin
- In healthy or normal people, very little amount of bilirubin is excreted in urine (about 0/02mg/dl)which cannot be measuring or measured by conventional methods
- Urobilinogen and bilirubin testes are used to interpret the state of liver disease

- Levels of these two substances can be very helpful to diagnosis of different types of jaundice (hepatitis)
- Blirubin + Diazo salt → Azobilirubin→Urobilinogen + Diethylaminobenzaldehyde colored complex

| urobilinogen | bilirobin | Types of jaundice |
|---|---|---|
| increased | negative | Pre-liver (hemolize) |
| Normal- increase | positive | Liver(hepatocellular disease) |
| reduced | positive | Post-liver (fibrosis, block, cholorocinoma) |

Table8: types of jaundice and associated whit bilirubin and urobilinogen

Pre liver: due to hemolysis, if RBC became high and then will be lysis Converts to bilirubin.

Post liver: due to block of liver duct or live cancer

**Confirmatory test:**
The erlikh test is used to confirm of urobilinogen test

Ikto test: confirmatory test for bilirobin

Usually urine strip are sensitive to 5mg/dl conjugated bilirubin

The false positive cases are cause or created by drugs such as chlorpromazine, fnaze and pyridine

Remaining of sample in front of light(sun, fluorescent) may be causes negative false answer

Urine ascorbic acid directly the reacted whit diazo and creates the colorless combination

The test Sensitivity in low temperature reduces

If only was consider the measurement of urine bilirubin, use of commercial diazo pill is recommended

The sensitivity of this tablets is 4 times more urine strip

If the check of bilirubin and urobilinogen is important, thus the sample should = = = remained in dark place

## Causes an increase and decrease urobilinogen:
Decrease: 1) sever urine acidosis   2) complete obstruction of bill

3) Board antibiotic therapy

Increase: 1) sever alkaline urine or sever urine alkaline

2) Liver damage   3) fever   4) Siros   5) viral liver hepatitis

6) Hemolytic anemia   7) tissue bleeding

$H^+$ ion = = react whit bromothymole blue and creating the or a color

$X^+$ + Polymethyl vinyl ether / maleicAnhydride → $X^+$ - polymethyl vinylEther / malic anhydrde + $H^+$

Relationship of specific gravity is inverse whit urine volume, = = =

Did or don't check = = = = = = specific gravity = = = urine strip

## Ketonuria:

Keton bodies → betahidroxybotiric acid

If or when keton concentration of blood higher than 70mg/dl = = = ketonuria

Diabetes mellitus inability to use of glucose can be seen = = =

Inadequate intake of carbohydrate, can be seen in starvation, diet, exercise and cold

Loss of carbohydrate = =observed due to frequent vomiting (pregnancy)

Impaired digestion: method of measuring ketone bodies on urine, called rothera test = = = = = are creates purple

In urine for detection of cystein = = use syanitroproside

In urinary strip Ketone bond, most sensitive part of mixture and chemical substances

Wrong remaining sample= = = = and creates false positive answer

Some drug such as pensylamin and captoril makes or creates false positive answer or response

Aceto acetic acid + Nitroprusside → Colored complex

## PH:

Used to diagnosis or recognize lung or kidney disease

Impaired of ph = shown impaired of lung or kidney

Used to diagnosis the type of crystal

Amorphous phosphate and amorphous urate are same

Amorphous phosphate precipitate

In alkaline PH and amorphous urate precipitate in acidic PH

The issue for RBC dissolving → (high PH)

Correct answer for specific gravity → (high PH)

The range of PH usually 4-9

Unsuitable usages of strips lead to separation of acidified buffer from protein bad and causing the contamination of PH band

## Dual detector system:

Methyl red → low PH, high concentration

Bromthymol blue→ high PH, low concentration

Reason of increase or decrease PH:

Increase: vegetarian food, chronic renal failure, urinary infection, urinary retention, = = =, respiratory disease whit hyperventilation

Decrease: meat food, diabetes, = vitamin c, starvation, dehyritaion, respiratory disease whit = co2, presence of blood in urine

= = - are sensitive to hematuria, hemoglobinuria and mioglobinuria

Distinguish mematuria from hemoglobinuria is urine transparency

To distinguish mioglobinuria from hemoglobinuria, should be measured plasma enzyme CK, LDH and heptaglobin

Due to the precipitation = = = ==

Ascorbick acid- sodium hypochlorite- bacterial praxidase- false positive

Blood, sugar, bilirubin → ascorbick acid caused false negative result

Haptoglobolin, CK, LDH of plasma increased in mioglobiniuria

Sodium hypochlorite = = = = = = = = == = == = = =

**Blood in urine:**

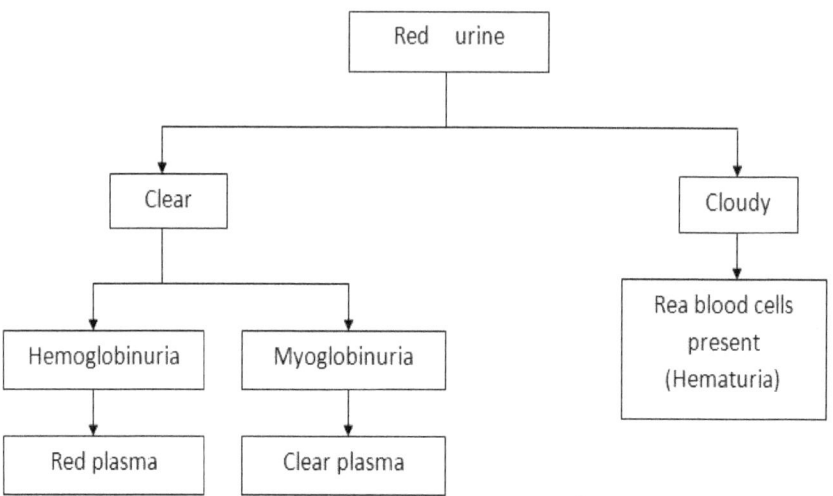

Consumption of beet → = = = = and makes also false response or answer

## proteinuria

| protein | Total === | Daily maximum |
|---|---|---|
| albumin | 40 | 60 |
| Tom horsfal | 40 | 60 |
| immunoglubin | 12 | 24 |
| Secreted IgA | 3 | 6 |
| Other protein | 5 | 10 |
| Total | 00 | 100 |

Table9: proteinuria

Distinguish of hematuria, hemoglobinuria, myoglobinuria

| State | RBC | Hb | mb |
|---|---|---|---|
| strip | + | + | I |
| Presence of RBC in urine | + | Negative or low | Negative or low |
| Appearance of urine | Dark red | Light red | Brown red light |
| Appearance of plasma | normal | Red pink | normal |
| CPK | normal | = == | = == |
| LDH | normal | increase | increase |
| LD1-LD2 | normal | increase | normal |
| LD4-LD5 | normal | increase | increase |

Table10: distinguish of hematuria, hemoglobinuria, myoglobinuria

There is = = fluid in glomerular membrance that called sialic acid have been negative charged . sialic acid is comprised by pyruvate + manose amin and it is 9 carbonate. Proteins have or have negative charge and sialic acid also have negative charge, so + repulsion, that causes the protein doesn't = in the urine

If sialic acid lost the negative charge = =small protein such as albomin == nephritic syndrome

Pre renal proteinuria: = = = increase of small plasma protein that pass from glomerular barrier.

When these proteins reach in to normal range proteinuria will disappear

The reason of this = = = == is hemoglobiuria mioglubinoria and multiple myeloma

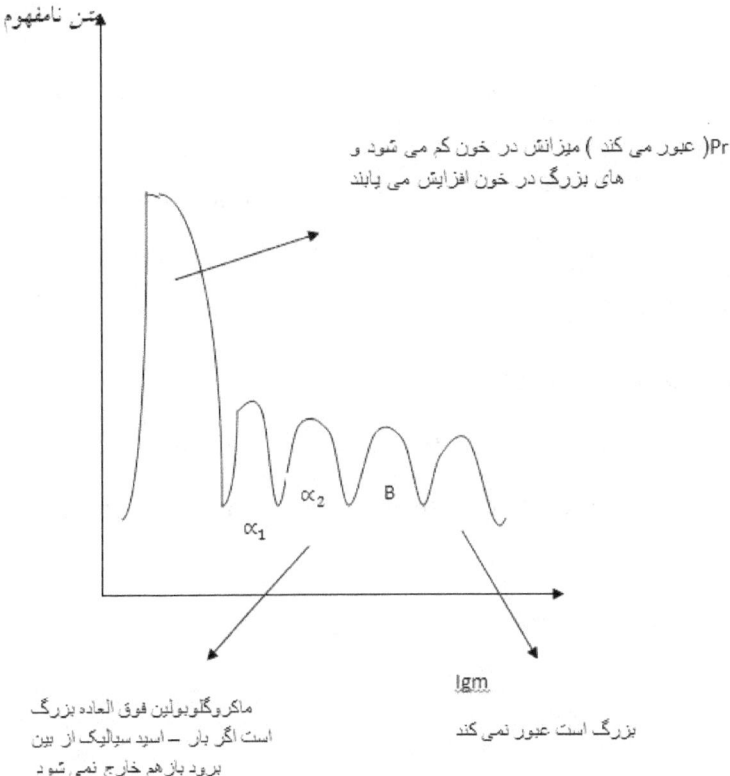

### Renal proteinuria:

As or by glomerular, tubular or the both can be seen

If glomerular barrier are or is damage large amount of plasma protein = =

Any disorder that change the negative charge of glomerular barrier causing albuminuria

Other proteins such as alpha 1 antitrypsin, transferin,..., can be seen in the urine that change negative charge of glomrular

Post renal proteinuria:

This type of proteinuria have a different factors such as pelvic inflammatory, prostitutes, urinary tract, external genital inflammatory menstrual blood protein, serum protein = = = = = = =

Albumin test → esbbach

Urine protein test or test of urine protein:

Urine strip = = = = more sensitive than other proteins

Globulin, buns jons and mokoprotein indistinguishable by urine strip

Confirm of stripe test done whit sediment test

| Confirmatory test SSA | | |
|---|---|---|
| Result of test | Value quality | Value quantity |
| No turbidity | - | <5mg/100 |
| Slight turbidity | Trace | 20mg/100 |
| Turbidity without granulation | + | 50mg/100 |
| Turbidity and granulation | ++ | 200mg/100 |
| Turbidity, granulation and flocculation | +++ | 500mg/100 |
| Sediment === | ++++ | 1000mg/100 |

Table11: confirmatory test SSA

Over and top of the +2, we have proteinuria

|  | SSA | strip |
|---|---|---|
| = alkaline urine | - | + |
| drug | + | - |
| Radiographic material | + | - |
| turbidity | + | - |

Tabl12: compared of false positive answer

Table13: mechanism of reaction

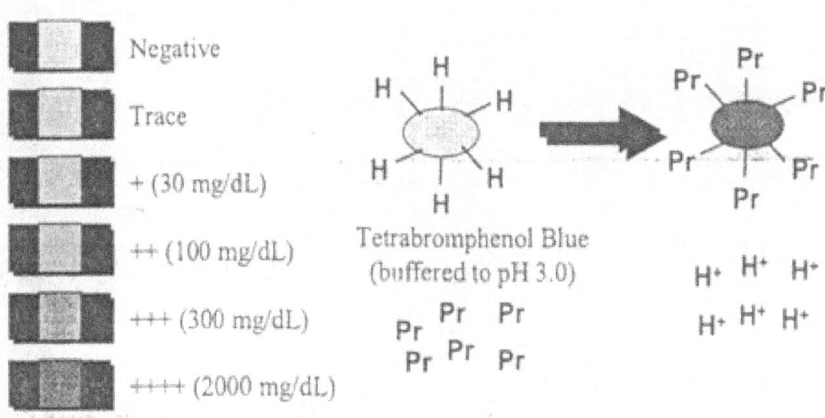

### Nitrite in urine:

Usually bladder and urine are sterile because of regular stream of urine

Anything that the urine stream are stop or slow, causing climber urinary infection

Urinary infection sometimes or often asymptomatic, in that case nitrite test is device for diagnosis of disease

Nitrate→ nitrite

Effective factor in nitrite test: remaining sample in bladder = = =enough time

Type of bacteria have = = = properties

Diet = === == = =

1) Nitrite + p – arsenilic acid ⟶ diazo compound

Diazo compound + Tetrahydrobenzoquinolinol ⟶ colored complex

2) Derivatized pyrrole amino acid ester ⟶ 3- hydroxyl 5- phnyl pyrrole

3) Hydroxyl - 5- phnyl pyrrole + diazo salt ⟶ colored complex

| Cause | Nitrite | Leukocyte esterase |
|---|---|---|
| infection | + | + |
| Immune suppress people | + | - |
| Exercise, inflammatory disease, trikomonase, clamidia | - | + |

Table14: discrepancies leukocyte esterase and nitrite

There are 3 type of parasite in urine: 1)trichomonas vaginalis → = =

2) eksio

3) Schistosoma hematobyom

The most appropriate sample of urine is sample of first morning or the first morning sample of urine is the most appropriate sample

= = =, acidosis PH of sample

Alkaline urine whit low specific gravity should be studied immediately

Suitable volume to review of deposition is 12ml (10-15ml)

6ml urine in children is acceptable

=== ====   === number of elements

Sample that = = = = = = without condensing and centrifuge. but should be noted did not centrifuge

Urine centrifuge done = = 2000-3000rpm

Urine centrifuge should be check whit in low power field and high power

= == = = == =====

The number of elements in the sediment to determine most be count 10 field then = == =

Low magnification used to counting of cylinders and high magnification used to counting of cells

The edge of coverslip or slid should be further investigated = = =

= = = =

Report of the element sediment == == = = =

As the number such as RBC report or report of RBC 20/10= 2 => RBC = 2-3

As the rare, few, moderate, number (plenty)

Urine of first morning by respiratory apnea = === = acidosis

In normal state PH of urine or urine PH is acidic but the fist morning is = ===

Acidic urine isn't appropriate for cytology = = = ==

Urine low volume of children in chemical test = = but the other test sach as count of RBC and WBC = ==

= = = = = = = = = = == =

One drop of cell release on slide and studied 10 fields


### RBC in urine:

In fresh urine, they are smooth and = = =

Originating any portion of urinary tract (glomerul and urinary tract)

There isn't RBC in urine of normal people

Bleeding of kidney or kidney bleeding shown or signature that increases of the number of RBC with cylinder

Increase the number of RBC without cylinder and protein associated whit bleeding == = = and menstrual contamination

Presence of more than two RBC called hematuria

Glomerular (RBC) = =: excreted from glomerul

Non-glomerular (same RBC): excreted from outside of glomerul

Pressure to or on RBC excreted causing different forms

Biochemical test ==:

1) Benzedine test: there are = test and benzedine identifier

2) occulate test: alcohol pyramydine, acetic acid, hydrogen peroxide creates = === (presence of ascorbic acid makes or create interfere)

Ascorbic acid in normally stat are or is dissolve in water (so, excreted from urine ==)

Match or equal whit chemical test:

If urine chemical test are positive by blood, but = = = in sediment, Probably, RBC lyses occurred in due to be dilute or alkaline urine, this subject can be occurred by presence of myoglobin and microbial peroxides in the urine.

== ==== ======= === ==

If PH of urine was alkaline, RBC have been lyses

Urine strip also == = colored whit myoglobin, hemoglobin

What hemosiderine and = = = urine stripe ?

== == = == = =========================== =
===================== ========= ===============
==== ===============

Hemosiderin is detect by Ross test (Ross water reaction)

15ml of urine were centrifuged. The supernatant = == discard, remaining sample were = suspend in the mixture of 5ml potassium ferosyanid 2% and 5ml HCL, = = and then centrifuged,   ======

HAM test is other method which = == == = = and added one drop of ammonium sulfate = = = = = = = =

Why excreted = = = night = = When iron of body is too much, stored in liver as hemosiderune. When we haven't muscle activity or activity of muscle, execratory pathway = =, then we have excretion of hemosiderin

RBC in urine:

Urine hemoglobin in sample that lyses should be more than 10/mg  = == == =

= = = == = = = smoking, hard exercise, illness(such as glomerulonephritis, pyelonephritis, renal tumors and renal stone) anti-coagulant, some antibodies (sulfonamide) as well as =====

The distance between slide and cover ship must be 10mm

Size of RBC: micro site (small)   termosite   macrosite (large)

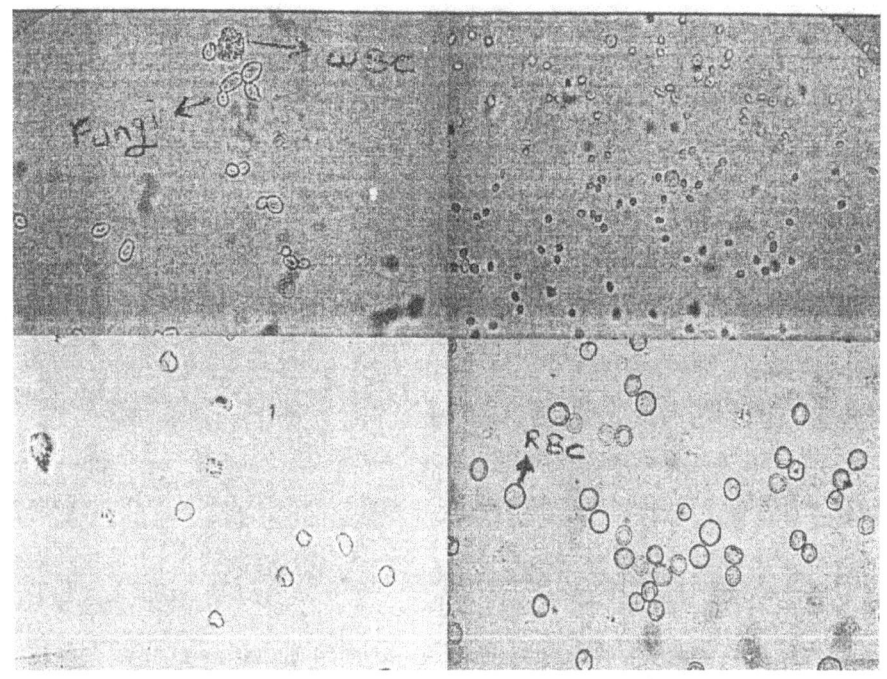

Future1: RBC, WBC and mushroom in urine

### WBC in urine

- Existence of more than 4 WBCs in the urine is called pyuria./ **[Increased number of WBCs (mainly neutrophils more than 5/hpf) in urine is known as pyuria]**
- When urinary tract infections occur, Neutrophils are in clumps.
- Sometimes after centrifugation the WBCs (tend to) stick together due to **inappropriate homogenization/improper homogenization,**
-
- The existence of WBC cylinder and granular cylinder with each other **Indicate the infection of upper urinary tract /Indicate that urinary tract infection is high.**
  • In this case the amount of Pr is high
- In Lower urinary tract infection the number of WBCs in urine sediment increases, but there is no cylinder (in it).( the amount of Protein is low)
- leukocytesare lysed in the urine very fast.This factor is the main reason for the possible difference between microscopic examination and chemical testing of leukocyte esterase.
- If in microscopic analysisthe number of leukocyte esteraseis less thanthe number of WBCs, the urine sediment WBCs areprobably not neutrophils.To **distinguish/**

**differentiate**WBC from epithelial cellsUse 2% acetic acid andan aqueous solution containing 5% iodine.

If the number of one type of WBCs is high,we will see clumps too. But if you see a clump because of mistakes made at work,single types of WBCs is low too.

**Pyelonephritis**:upper urinary tract infection.

**Cystitis:** Lower Urinary Tract Infections

**Mycosis [(fungal infection)]:** excessive fungi in the urine

- The number of WBCs increases almost in all patients with kidney disease.

- Infectious disease: pyelonephritis, cystitis, prostatitis, urethritis

- Noninfectious diseases, lupus nephritis, dehydration, fever

- **Trichomoniasis/ Trichomonas**and mycosis.

- Trichomoniasisand mycosis Indicate contamination of the urine by vaginal discharge**/ is primarily an infection of urinary tracts and in women with vaginal discharge** and**usually** indicate a vaginal infection.

- Trichomoniasis in men indicates an infection of the urinary tract which is transmitted to them from their wives.

- Eosinophils in the urine is often a sign of acute nephritis.

## WBC در ادرار

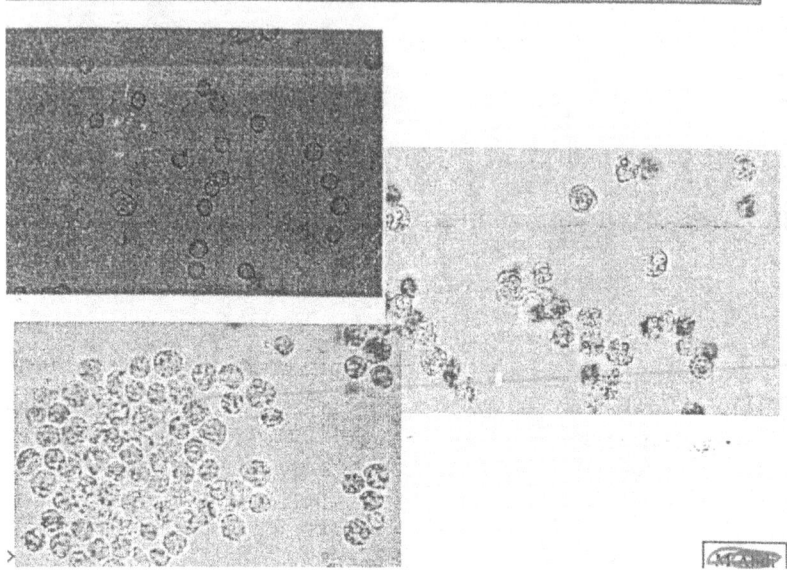

Figure 2: [Different]**types of WBCs/Forms of WBC** in the urine

Epithelial cells
- **Squamous**
- **Transitional**
- **Renal Tubulat**

**Squamous:**

- The most common type of epithelial cells is squamous.

- Thepresence of **a small** number of epithelial cells in the urine is not necessarily a sign of disease.

- It(Disease) may be caused because **the older cells die off in front and are cast offas new ones are formed behind./the oldercells get detached** .


- is the largest type of cell
- Old cells are constantly get detached and **whisked away/are excreted**
- Large numbers of these cellsin women's urineindicate contamination of the urine by vaginal discharge.
- The presence of these cells in uncircumcised males **is indicative of sample contamination/may represent contamination of the sample.** .The presence of epithelial cells in the urine indicates that sample was taken from first **part/ portion** of the urine, because they cover the outer part of urinary tract(outer foreskin/ urethra) .

**Transitional**

- transitional epithelial cells
- from the renal pelvis to the urethra
- Can be round , tailed , polygonal or pear-shaped
- In healthy people, sometimes because of**detachment of old cells**only a few of these cellscan be seen(mostly **cells of surface and rounded type/rounded surface cells** ).

- There is an increase in the number interstitial cells in the urinary tract infections.
- If exfoliated layer of cells are observed in the urine and if there's no catheter, the Patient should be examined for **(potential)** malignancy.

(Cells) are Round and elliptical because of **exfoliation/detachment** of old cells

In necrosis the **upper renal tract/upper urinary tract** is Pear-shaped or polygonal shape with tails

is indicative of the upper renal tract cancer

in infection

**Renal tubulat /Renal tubular epithelial cells:**

- The presence of a small numbers of renal tubular epithelial cells Indicate the replacement of new cells.
- An increase in the number of cells indicates [the possibility of] tube defects.
- Pyelonephritis, acute tubular necrosis, salicylate intoxication, and kidney transplant rejection.
- The number of these cells in the urine of infants is greater than that of children and adults.
- Renal tubular epithelial cells filled with fat droplets are called oval fat bodies.

OFB is **an indicator of/ sign of** renal tubular cells death and acute [kidney] injury.

After deposition of plasma, severe proteinuria will be found in urine.

This type is more common in babies' kidneys growth.

In diabetes in which acute kidney failure occurs, proteinuria is very high and following by that the **fat/lipid** is also excreted. They are drawn inside by tubular cells andare accumulated, so OFB **forms/occurs.**

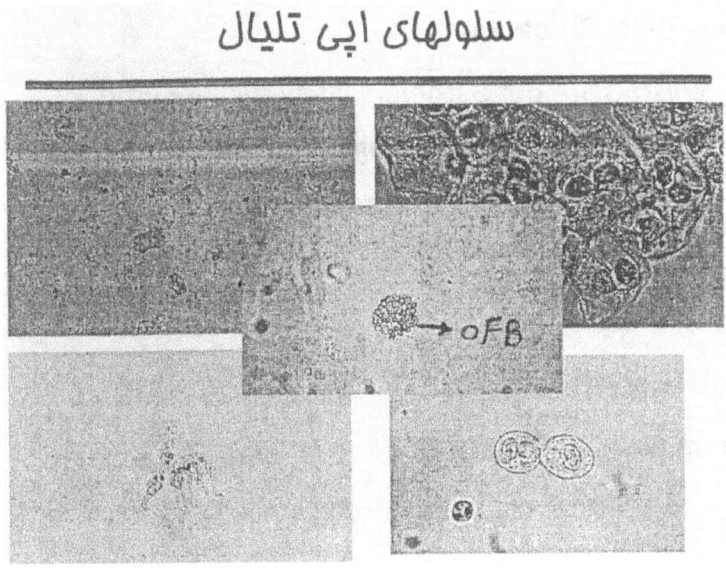

Figure 3: **[Different] types of /Forms of**OFB in urine

- The vaginal cream causes lipid to be **found/seen** in the urine.
- The presence of sperm in the urine is a sign of prostate problem.

## Urinary crystals

- Urine crystals result from deposition of material **due to/caused by** changes in properties of materials or their saturation in urine.
- Fresh and normal urine does not **contain/have** crystals.
- (Analysis of) urinary crystals are reported based on their appearance and the PH of urine.
- Most crystals are not pathological, however, **some crystals are indicative of the pathological process/ some crystals can be pathologically relevant in certain circumstances.**

Uric acid crystals

**Calcium oxalate crystals**

**1-    Calcium Oxalate Dihydrate**

- These crystals are colorless and have a (characteristic) octahedral or envelope shape.

**2-    Calcium oxalate monohydrate**

- **(Calcium oxalate dihydrate)** are usually spindle shaped.

This crystal usually occurs in people who consume a high-oxalate diet, and pathologically in people who have kidney stones and in patients with acute renal failure due to effects of ethylene glycol.

- **Red urine indicates the presence of crystal.** These crystals disappear at 37 °C and should not be reported.

**Uric acid crystals**

- Pathologic; kidney stones, acute crystal nephropathy
- The presence of these crystals in the urinary sediment does not necessarily mean the formation of crystals in the urinary tract.
- These crystals can also **form/occur** after urination.
- These crystals are related to PH and temperature as well as the presence of urea-degrading bacteria in the urine.
- These crystals have different sizes and shapes. They can be needle-shaped, rosette, diamond and Hexagonal shaped.

In cystinuria in addition to cysteine lysine, arginine, and ornithine are also excreted.

- In contrast to **(polymorphic)** urate crystals, cystine crystals are monomorphic, colorless hexagonal plates [which look similar to benzene rings.]
- These crystals are mainly found in the acidic **environments/conditions** and patients with cystinuria.

- *Triple phosphate crystals (struvite)* **look like coffin lids/resemble coffin lids** *and* ***occur/ form in in an Alkaline environment / require an alkaline environment to form.***

- <u>***Triple phosphate crystals (struvite) are coffin lid shaped/Triple phosphate crystals have a unique "coffin lid" appearance***</u>*and* *are more likely to develop if the pH value is alkaline./ usually exist in an alkaline pH/ basic pH* <u>*conditions/environment*</u>*.*

-

These crystals are found in patients with urinary tract infections caused by **urea degrading bacteria/ urease-producing organisms**(such as Proteus Mirabilis), and also in people with Struvitekidney stones.

In most cases, the presence of these crystals is associated with the presence of leukocyte bacteria in the urine.

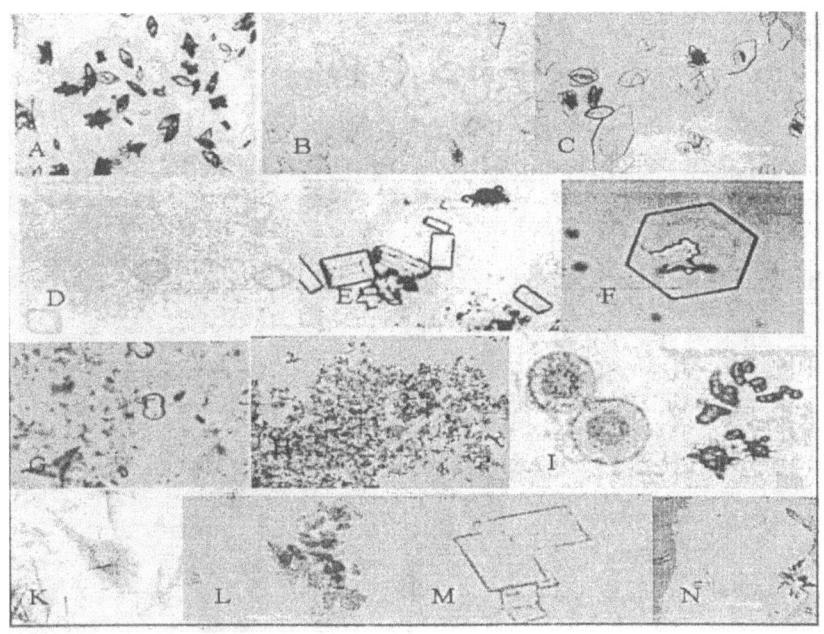

Table 15: **Urine crystals / Urinary crystals**

- Triple phosphate crystals (usually) exist in an alkaline pH.

**Amorphous**

Basic(alkaline) pH        Amorphous phosphates

Acidic pH                 Amorphousurate

- **Red blood cells lyse in water / RBC is lysed by water**
- In the environment in which the Sg is high, the RBCs become wrinkled.
- Has central core tubular epithelial cells and **the smallest interstitial ratio/the smallest proportion of interstitial.**

**Urinary casts:**

The absence of casts does not rule out renal disease.

- Urinary casts are cylindrical structures composed mainly of mucoprotein (the Tamm-Horsefallmucoprotein)     Tamm – Horsefall

- Site/place of secretion

• loop of Henle, Tubular crystals, collecting ducts,

- influencing Factors on the formation of cylinders

• Urination stop, increase in acidity, the concentration of solutes in the urine, the existence of ionic compoundsor abnormal protein.

Cast formation

- Damage to cast cells causes different types of casts. [ **(Their occurrence indicates mild or extensive tubule cells damage)]**

- waxy cast -Granular cast - Cellular Cast

- presence of casts in urine sediment

- the time of staying in the place of **formation/sedimentation**

- Place of Formation

**Reporting and interpretation of casts**

- Reports based on the Number per LPF (lox) and the type of casts

Waxy Casts, 5 – 10/LPF

- In healthy individuals there are few or does not exist entirely.

*[Waxy casts can be found in persons with advanced kidney disease]*

**Granular and hyaline**

- The absence of casts does not rule out renal disease
- **Though** the presence of a large number of casts is suggestive of **kidney/renal** diseases. (mostlyacute diseases)**however,** it is not a reliable marker for Prognosis.

**Cast = Silandr**

**Cylinder-like structures with parallel**


Becausethe **urinary tract/ ureters** are cylindrical in shape,these objects take the form of cylinderwhichare called "cylinder".

Only hyaline casts are considered normal.

**When the hyaline casts begin to pick up RBC, WBC, EP cells, they become cellular casts./ when RBC, WBC, EP cells adhere to the surface of a hyaline cast , it becomes cellular cast.**The material damages due to(due to urine stops in the **tube/urethra/**)causes granular casts. As these damages increase over time,they becomewaxy casts which indicate serious kidney problems. The presence of these casts indicates kidney problems.

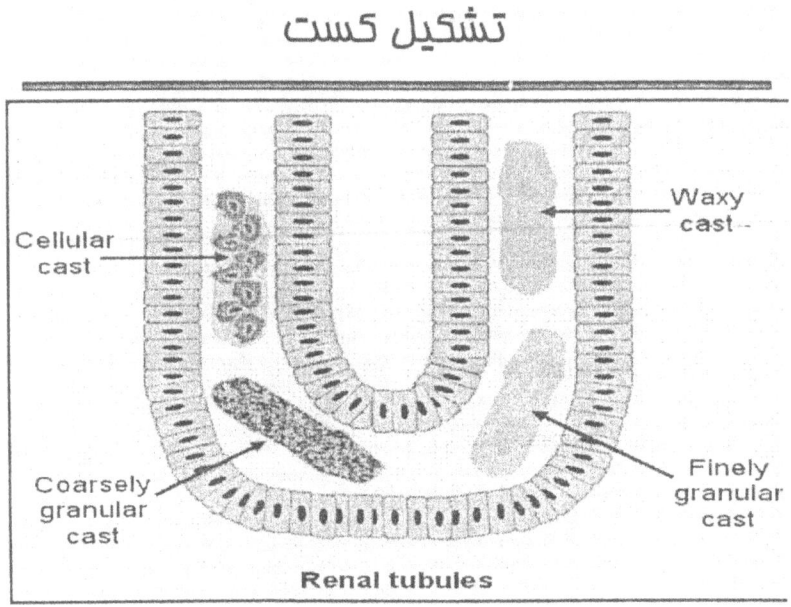

Figure 6: cast formation

Whichcast **can be/is**excreted in the chronic kidney disease?

1) Hyaline cylinders can be seen in even the mildest **kind/type** of renal disease.

2) Cylinder cellular(EP) is seen in severe chronic kidney diseasein which tubular damage**is accompanied by/ is associated with** glomerular injury.

3) Waxy casts can be found in **[persons with advanced kidney disease and] chronic kidney failure.**( also In Acute kidney disease).

- More granular cells will be excreted because it will befor a long time that Cellular has also been converted into a granular.

**Diagnosis of cast**

1) hyaline casts

2) Cellular castsRed blood cells (RBCs)**[, also called erythrocytes]**

White blood cells (WBCs)

Epithelial

3) granular casts
4) Fatty Casts
5) Waxy casts

**Hyaline Casts:**

- Hyaline casts are formed in the absence of cells**[(in the tubular lumen)]**.
- Hyaline casts are formed by Tamm Horsfall protein.

- Hyaline Casts are very difficult to distinguish/[ **Hyaline casts are difficult to see because of their low index of refraction**]

- Hyaline casts have parallel sides[ **with clear margin**] and blunted ends.

- Reduced lighting is essential to see hyaline casts in urine sediment.(by microscope)

- Normal **Hyaline Casts**are 0-1/LPF

- are pathologic

- Proteinuria (glomerulonephritis)

- Proteinuria outside the kidney" (myeloma**)** [ /the **Proteinuria caused by diseases not involving the kidneys**]

- The deposits of Tamm-HorsfallPrincreases if the<u>**protein( Pr) amount rises/ protein level rises**</u>in renal tract.

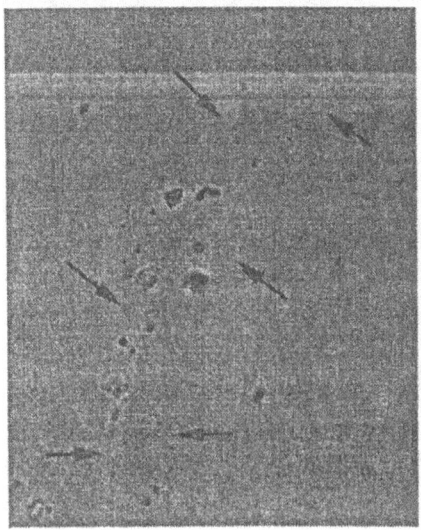 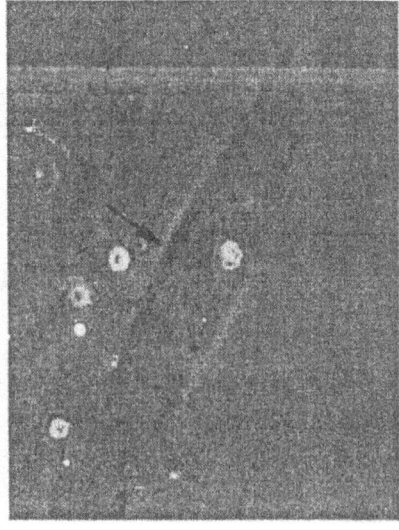

Cellular Casts:

- The gradual progression of diseases such as ischemia, infarction, Nefrotoksisitas.
- Degeneration and necrosis of tubular epithelial cells
- indicating acute tubular injury
- **Reduction/ Decrease** in urine output and secondary oliguria due to severe dehydration.

If blood does not reach the kidney for 10 seconds, kidney cells willbe destroyed, therefore ischemia occurs. Cells detach from wall andenter the tubules. It is tubular epithelial cell that become cast.

## Epithelial Cast

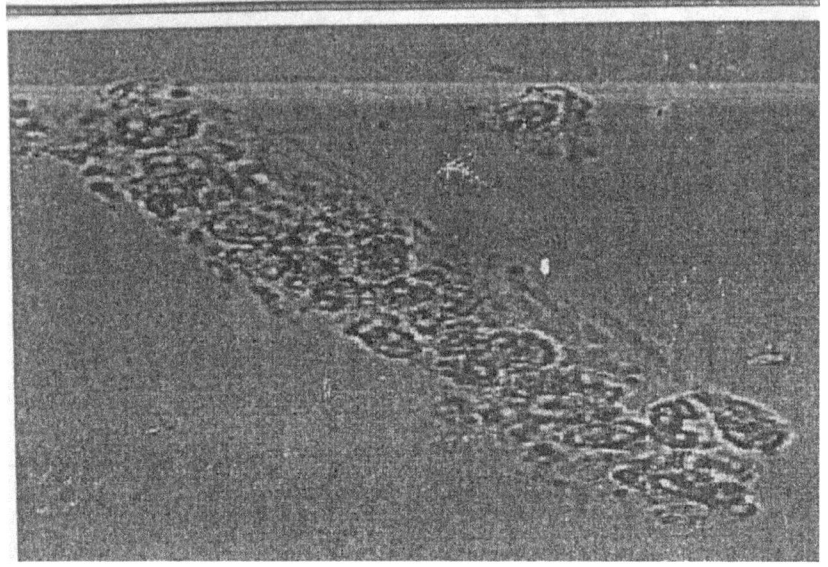

## RBC Cast

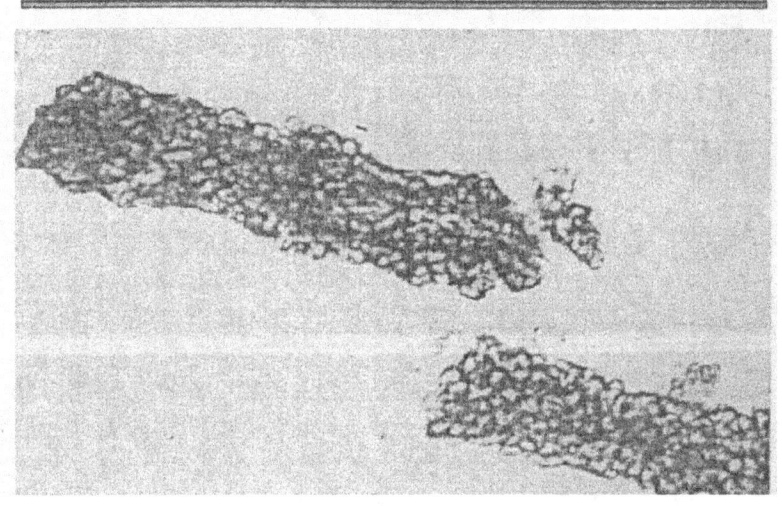

## WBC Cast

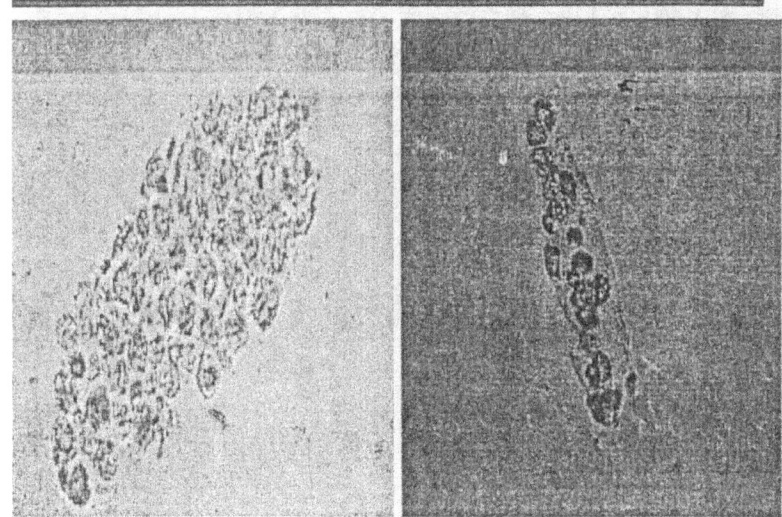

Granular Cast

Classification of casts based on their texture

- Fine
- Coarse
- Cellular casts occur as a result of degeneration

Granular Casts

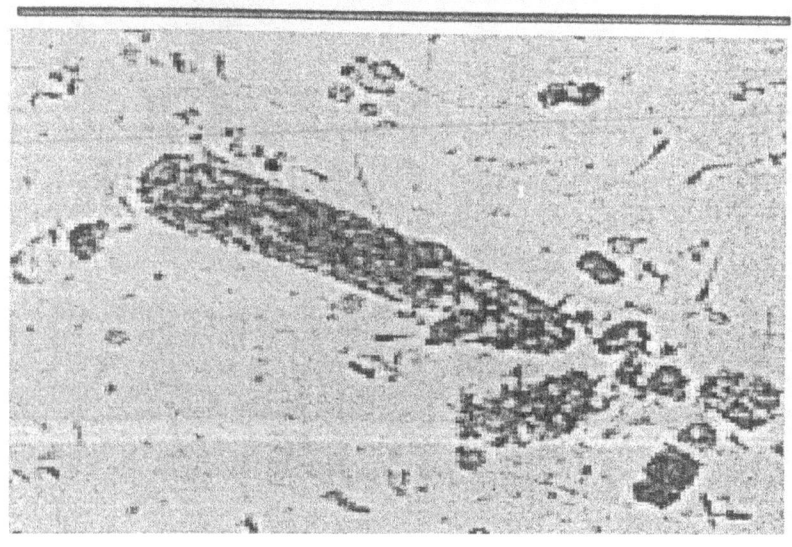

## Granular Casts

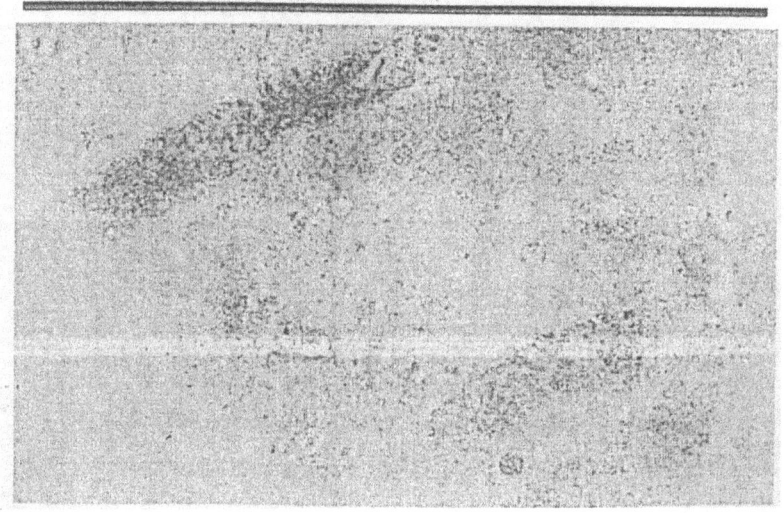

## Granular Casts

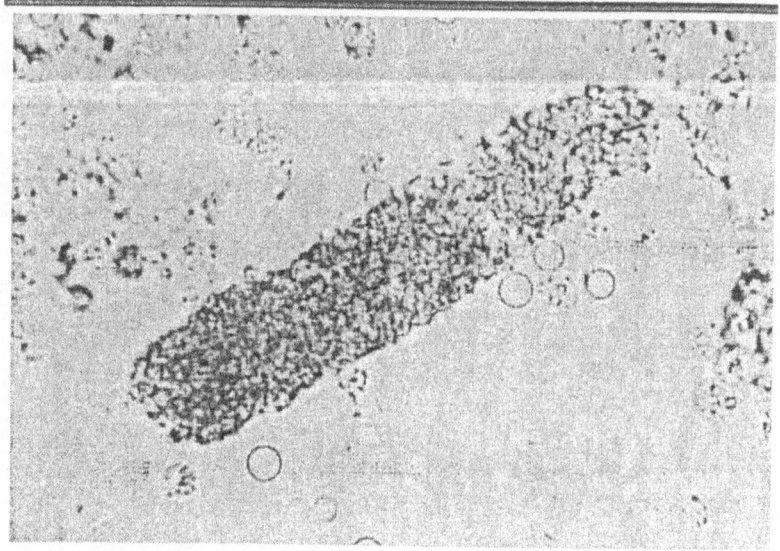

Figure 11: granular casts

Fatty Casts:

- contain lipid droplets
- are Often found in the urine containing lipid droplets

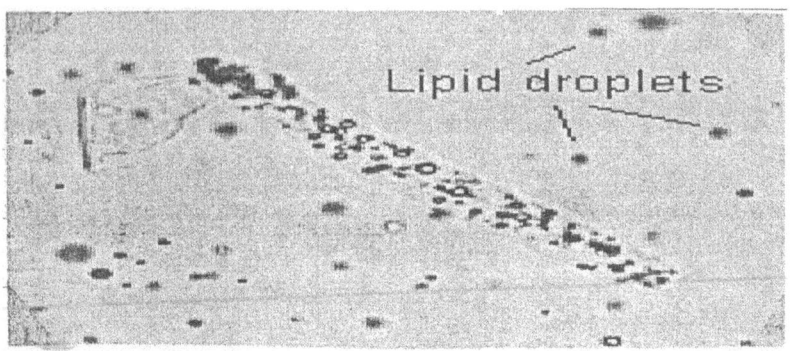

**Waxy Casts:**

- havesmooth surface and are capable of reflecting light.
- They commonly have squared off ends**, [as if brittle and ]easily broken/ and are brittle**

Indicator of chronic renal tubular damage

# Waxy Casts

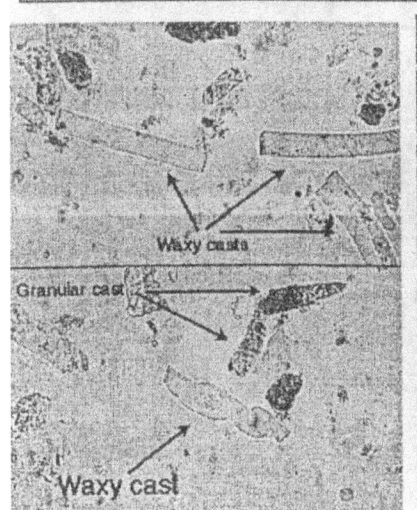
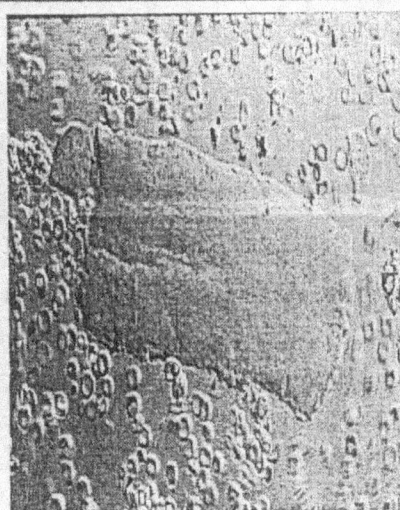

# Urinary Casts

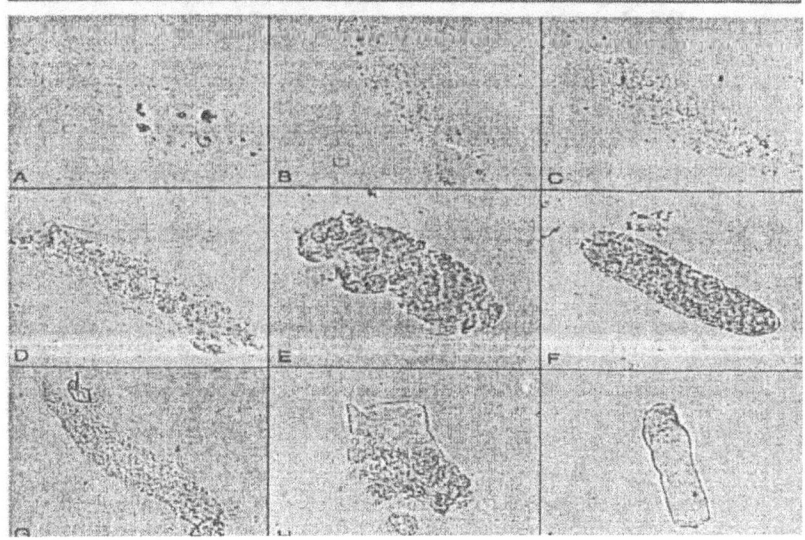

# Urinary Casts

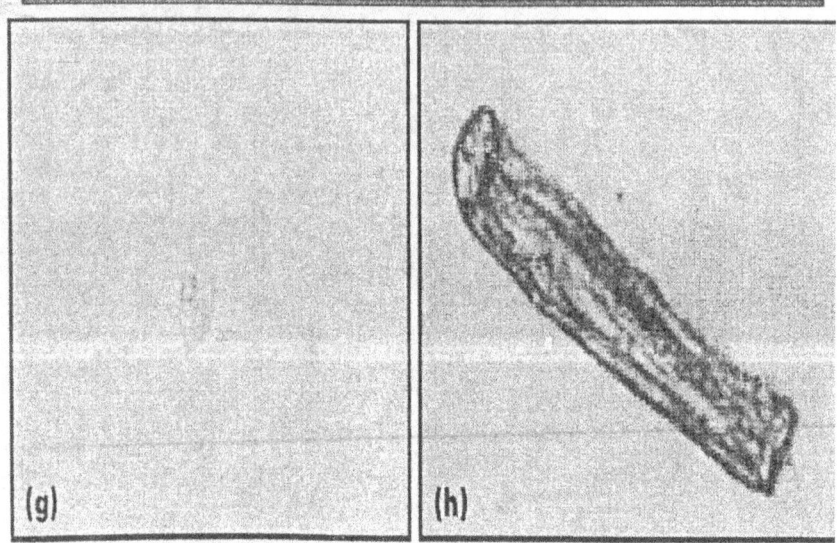

# Chapter 2

## Water and electrolytes

Blood gases and acid-base disorders and Laboratory studies show that the solid levels are higher for womenbecause they have a higher percentage of fat/lipid.

- **Membranes contain aquaporin/ there are channels or aquaporins in the[cell]membranes,** because the permeability of the membrane is unresponsive.

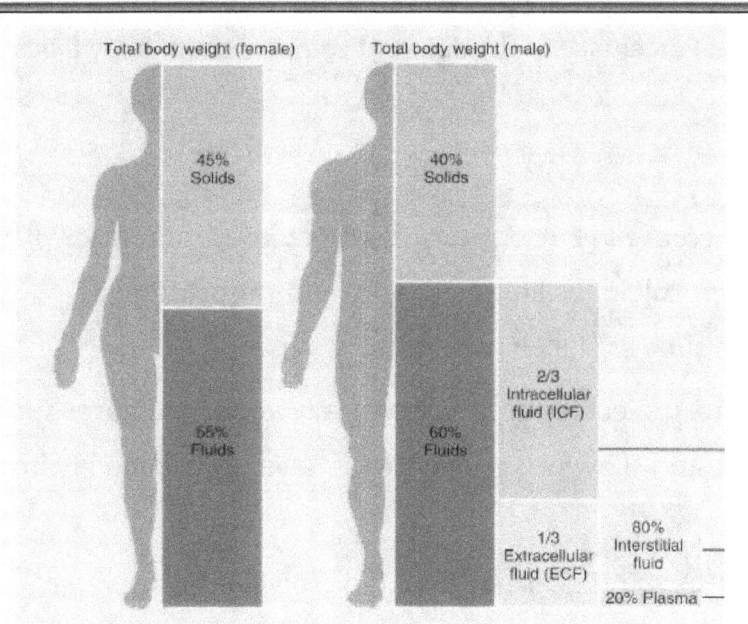

Figure14: Percentage of solids in men and women

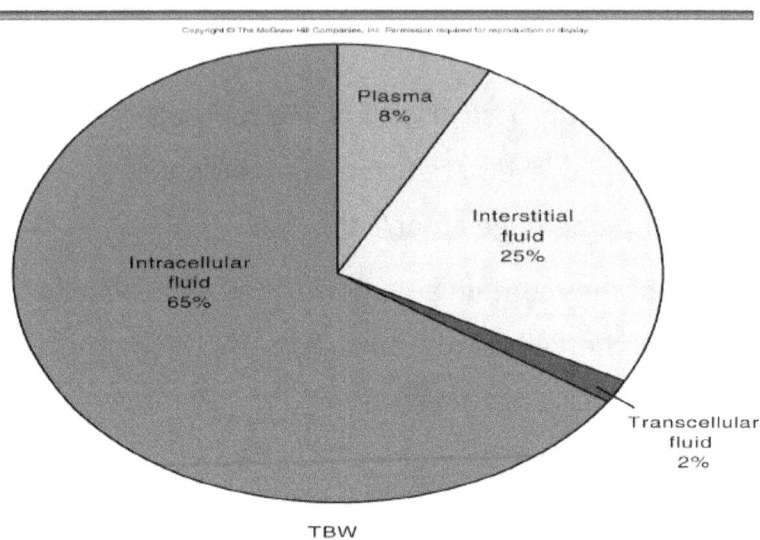

Figure 15: Percentage of the different components of body fluids

## Solubility

- Increase in Entropy **has the most important role/ plays important role** in facilitating the dissolution[process] of minerals such as NaCl in water.

- The molecules of the biologically important gases such as $CO_2$, $O_2$, and $N_2$ which are nonpolar have poor solubility in water.

- $NH_3$ and $H_2S$ are polar and dissolve easily in water

- Biological membranes are vulnerable to water. Passing of water across these membranes is determinedby the concentration gradient of electrolyte such as sodiumand by concentration of materials such as glucose and urea.

## Osmosis

Flow of water through a semipermeable membrane into a **region of higher solute concentration/region containing higher concentrations of dissolved materials** is called osmosis

Osmotic pressure: the pressure of the osmotic flow of water through a semi-permeable membrane into a **region of higher solute concentration /region containing higher concentrations of dissolved materials.** The osmotic pressure is measured by the van't Hoff equation: $\Pi = icRT$ Where R is the gas constant and T is the absolute temperature [of the gas] ."ic" represents osmolarity. Osmolarity is a product of the molar concentration of solute and the van't Hoff factor," I".

- Factor "I" is a measurement of the extent of dissociation.[/**number of ions formed by of dissociation of a solute molecule.** ]

- **This factor is a measurement of the extent of dissociation of the solute./ The van't Hoff factor is equal to how many particles(ions) the solute dissociates into.** For example, [NaCl dissociates into Na+ and Cl-,so ]the van't Hoff factor forNaClis 2and for Glucose, it is 1 [ **Glucose does not dissociate, so it's van't Hoff factor is 1**]

Osmotic pressure depends on the molar concentration [of the solute] and the number of particles **[in solution]**. For example, glucose and glycogen which are **heavy** yields 1 particle but NaCl which yields 2 particles, has higher osmotic pressure.

- Osmosis: water moves from areas of low <u>**particles/materials**[low solute concentration]</u> to areas of high <u>**particles/materials**[high solute concentration]</u> (are more concentrated).
- Isotonic; materials inside and outside the cells are in equilibrium.

**Hypertonic**: substances is greater outside the cell and water goes outside (flow out of the cell) /[**Solute concentration outside the cell is higher (less water)**]

**Hypotonic**: water move from outside to the inside of the cell

## Homeostasis

- The ability or tendency of an organism or cell to maintain the **state/ Composition** of internal environment despite a changing external environment.

- Proper distribution of water and maintenance of the proper concentration of electrolyte and PH level are essential for homeostasis.

- Regulation of body water balance

- Hypothalamic thirst-regulating mechanism, ADH, Evaporation through respiratory tract and sweating.
- Increase in Na leads to an increase in **[total]**body H2O.
- Increase in sodium leads to an increase in [the amount of] body water.
- Increase in excretion of fluids leads to dehydration.

When cells are dead, they equilibrate with their surroundings. Energy prevents the cells to reach equilibrium with their surroundings.

ADHis secreted from the **posterior pituitary (or neurohypophysis)gland**. Antidiuretic hormone = ADH

Arginine – vasopressin

AVP

- antidiuretic hormone:ADH

Sodium reduction: affects osmoreceptor and inhibits it, causes a decrease in the secretion of ADH and thirst,as a result, the excretion of water in urine is increased and body's water is supplied.

- Increase in sodium: Homeostasis **is[/may]** lostin patients with an increase in [total body] sodium. When Na increases,osmoreceptors (hypothalamus and cervical vessels) are stimulated and ADH is increased. It also affects the hypothalamus and the need for drinking water is stimulated. In thirsty, ADH affects the kidney proximal and the reabsorption takes place. And thus the amount of body water increases and homeostasis is compensated ( increase in آپویورین **type ii**)


- renin is secreted from ژوبستراگلومرول **part /[ Renin is secreted from juxtaglomerular kidney cells]**
- Angiotensin II is secreted by the lungs. Reabsorption of sodium, chloride and water and an increase in the secretion of H +.

## نقش سدیم در هومئوستاز آب

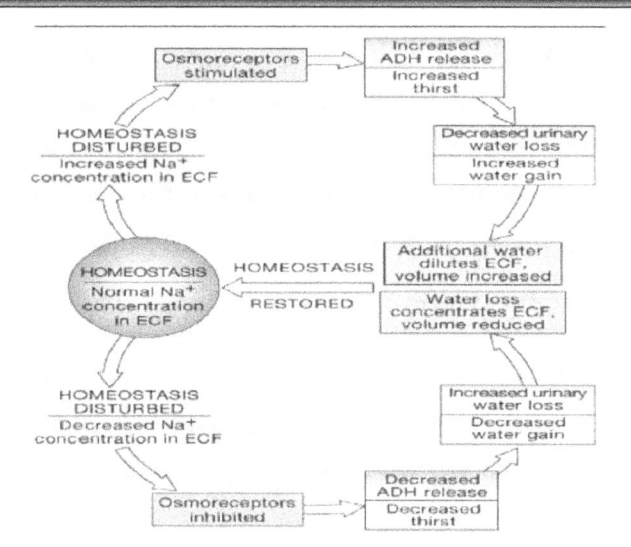

**Figure 19:** Role of sodium in **water/fluid** homeostasis (When homeostasis is established, the amount of sodium is normal)

**Pituitary gland (hypophysis)**

**Anterior** pituitary gland which produces and secrets its hormones

**Posterior** pituitary which stores and **secrets/release** hormones produced by the hypothalamus (secretes ADH and oxytocin)

Under usual conditions the ECF is normal.

- when ECF increases by the following 3 factors:

1- Increase in water

2- Increase in Na disrupted Homeostasis

3- Decrease in Na reabsorption

- causes blood and water volume to increase (arterial pressure increases), causes an increase in Np(natriuretic) secretion, (cause) a decrease in sodium reabsorption (This hormone play an auxiliary role).

peptid   natriuretic/ natrium+ Na+

examples:

BNP is secreted from the brain

ANP is **produced by/secreted from** the heart

1- causes a decrease in aldosterone secretion.

2- Reducing thirsty

3- decrease in ADH


**Drinking Water**

**Increase in ADH secretion**


**Receptor Deficiency**

**Deficiencies in aquaporin genes**


- causessodium and potassium to be reabsorbed. It is secreted from the adrenal(فوق كليه)

The renin-angiotensin system (RAS) causes a decrease in secretion. -------------a decrease in aldosterone secretion and ADH.Increase in K + causes this secretion.

- As aldosterone levels become low, sodium is excreted in the urine.

- when ECF decreases

1- **decrease in water/the amount of water decreases**

2- **decrease in Na+/the amount of Na decreases**

**Leads to Dehydration which is caused by an increase in Pr/Increase in Pr causes Dehydration to occur.** There are also Diarrhea or vomiting, a **drop/fall** in blood pressure and a **reduction/loss** in blood volume which increasesrenin(angiotensin) secretion.

Increase in aldosterone

Increase in ADH

Increase in reabsorption

The excretion of water from the body decreases.

Homeostasis returns to the normal state

**Water homeostasis**

- Fluid volume deficit may lead to hypotension (a **drop/fall** in blood pressure) , shock, freezing and death.The mechanisms by which water homeostasis **is maintained/ is achieved** are:

• Central diabetes insipidus; Disorder of ADH secretion, Pituitary(hypophysis) problem.

• Nephrogenic diabetes insipidus, insensitivity( of the kidneys or nephrons) to ADH

**Diabetes insipidus causes the excretion of more water./in patients with diabetes more water is excreted/.( blood)** sugar level is high, much water is absorbed andtherefore, ADH increases.

• PH and its biochemical effects (PH = -logH+)

- PH is a measure of the concentration of hydrogen ions in the environment.

- PH has effects on the structure and activity of macromolecules.

- The determination of blood and urine PH are used for medical diagnosis.

- Strong acids and bases dissociate completely in water.

RH ⇌ R- + H+ , [ RH ] = 0 K = [R- [] H+ ] / [ RH ], K⇌

Small percentage of weak acids and bases dissociate in water.

$RH \rightleftharpoons R^- + H^+$ , $K = [R^-][H^+] / [RH]$

- **acids and bases in biological systems usually have a k less than 1 /Generally K acids and bases in biological systems is a fraction smaller than 1.**
- Because the values of K for weak acids are very small, the PK is used instead. Most of the body's acids and bases are weak acids and bases.
- Most biological acids are polyvalent, so they have many different PK.

## PH measurement equations
Sorensen equation $PH = -\log[H^+]$

Henderson–Hasselbalch equation $PH = PK + \log[A^-] / [AH]$

یکپارچگی حجم آب و غلظت سدیم بمنظور حفظ هومئوستاز آب

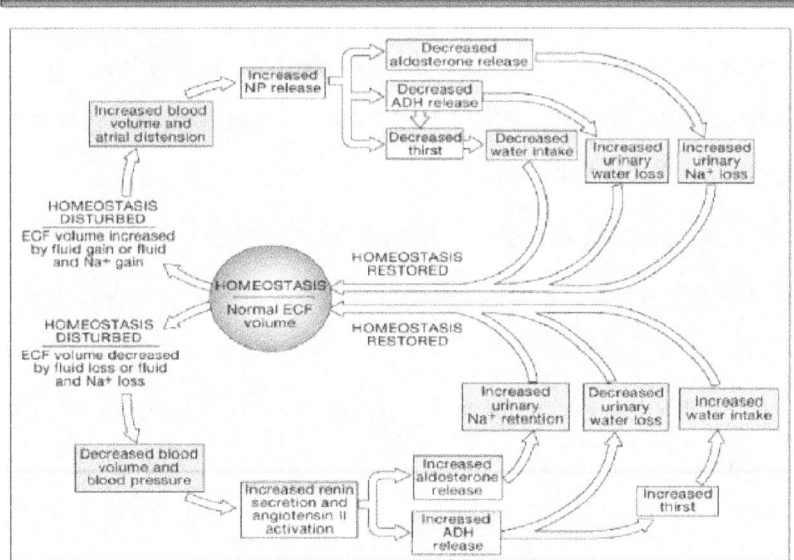

Figure 20:the integrity of the volume of water and Sodium concentration(in order) to maintain water homeostasis.

## سیستم بافری

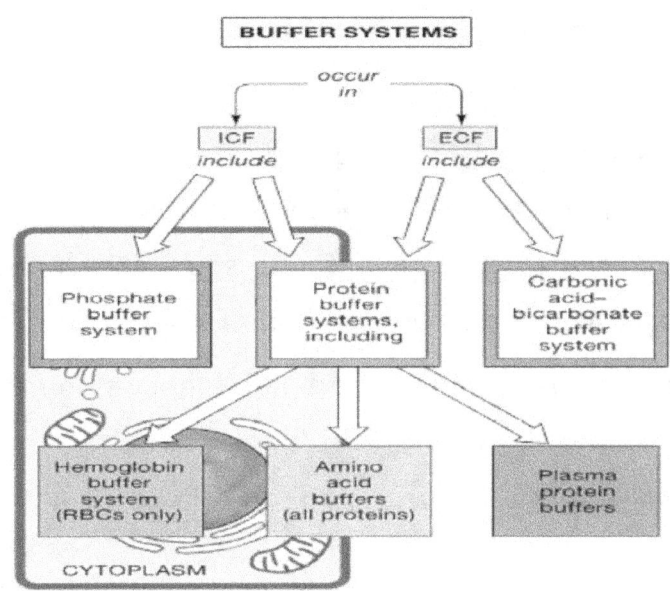

Figure 21: buffer system in the body

**Buffer and buffering action(features)**

- Tendency of avolume of solution to effectively resistchanges in PH ismore than the tendency of the amount of water **equal to its volume/with the same volume** to resist these changes. This resistance (to pH change) is called buffering action.

- **Physiological buffers**

- Phosphate, bicarbonate, Prs, Hemoglobin, calcium carbonate

- **three main mechanisms**

Buffering system

Respiratory system

Renal system

70 to 80 percent of the Prshave negative charge. The haemoglobin absorbs the H + ionsand acts as a buffer (to restore pH). **Calcium carbonate buffering is for bone**[ /Release of calcium carbonate from bone is a buffering mechanism.]

- Bicarbonate is the most important buffering system in the body

- Phosphate buffer ($H_2PO_4$ : $HPO_4$ ) is **only(mainly)** intracellular.

- $HCO_3-$ + $Na+$Alkalis storage which the body will release it whenever necessary.

- There is a special relationship between the $co_2$ pressure and plasma PH

- **Blood has a $PCO_2$ of 40-45/The $PCO_2$ of blood is 40-45, Body's PH is .57.4+-**

**$PCO_2$  40 - 45  Blood**

**PH    7.4 +- 0. 5  Body**

## سیستم بافری دی اکسید کربن-بی کربنات

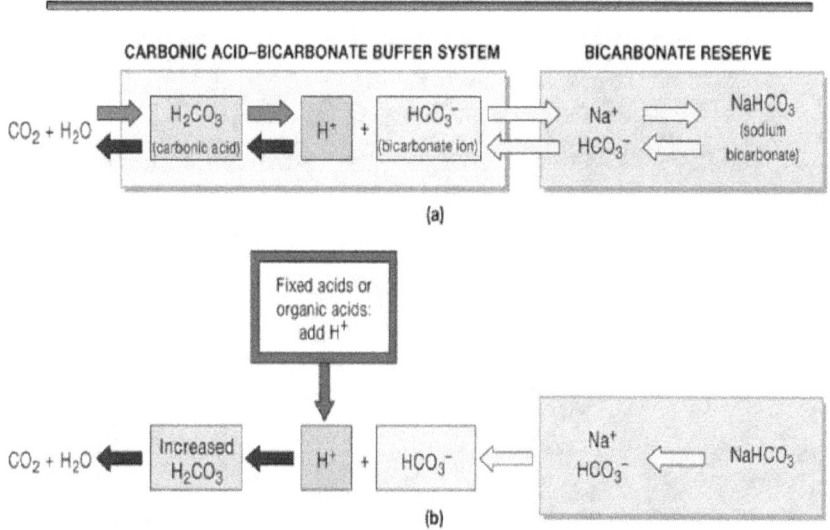

Figure22:Buffering system of carbon dioxide – bicarbonate

## ارتباط بین $P_{CO2}$ و pH پلاسما

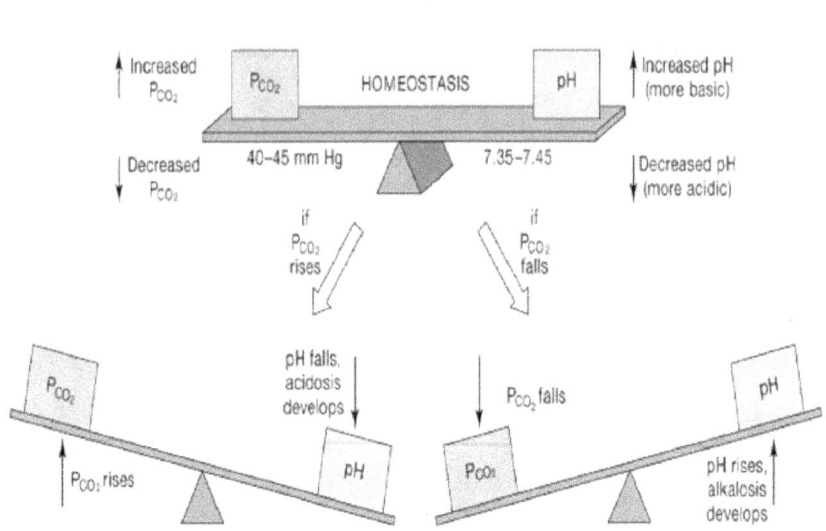

Figure 23: Relationship between the co2 and plasma PH

## ساختار نفرون های کلیوی

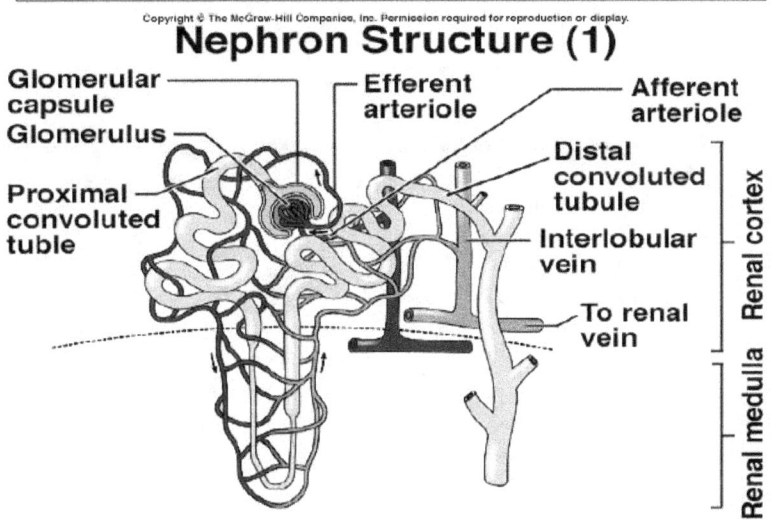

Figure 24: Structure of a Kidney Nephron

## توبول های کلیوی و تنظیم pH

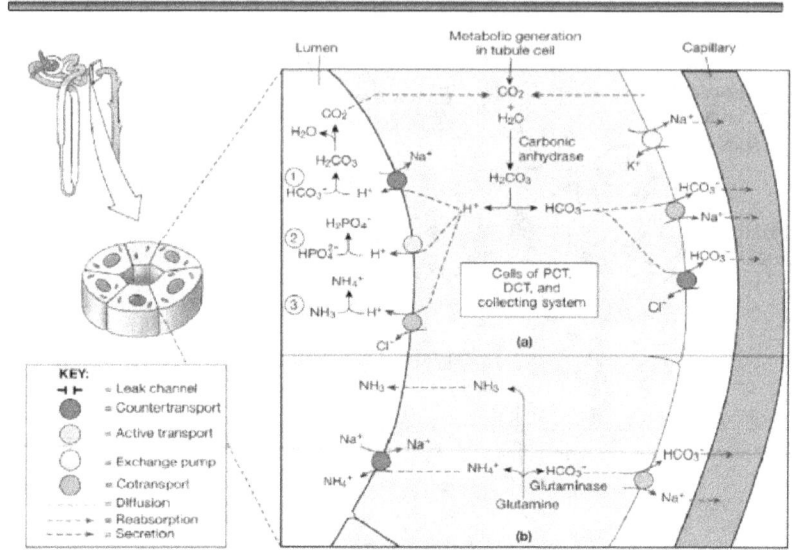

Figure 25: Renal tubules and PH regulation

Carbonic anhydrase

H2O + CO2 ←-----→ H2CO3

(Carbonic anhydrase) Through binding to the Band 3 exits RBC and goes into the lungs.(Which imports cl and exports HCO3 )/**absorb cl or give off HCO3**

**Kidney function:** Reduction of H + and restoration of HCO2

As H+ decreases pH increases, so H+ must be reduced(by the kidney) and The HCO2- of the body must be maintained.

➔ Ammonia is converted into urea in the liver/**The liver converts ammonia into urea.**

When H increases, ammonia goes into the kidney not into the liver. By absorbing H+ it is converted into ammonium ions and is excreted in the urine. (urinary ammonia buffer occurs in the acidosis state)

->Ammonia is highly neurotoxic, and with glutamic acid is in the state of glutamine in the blood and in this state goes to the liver and the kidney.

- The Other carrier is pyruvate which by absorbing NH2 +, is converted into alanine. Pyruvate also exists in muscles which absorbs NH2 + and in the state of alanine goes to the liver.

When H+ increases, ammonia goes into the kidney not into the liver. It is (then) converted into ammonium and is excreted in the urine.

The **role/function** of pyruvate

The absorption of ammonia and conversion of it to alanine (entering the liver)

pyruvate

ammonia-------------------➔alanine (entering the liver)

Acid-base imbalance

- Life continuesin the range of PH = 6/8- - 8
- Normal body pH is 7/35- 7/ 45

Table 16: acidosis and Alkalosis

| Alkalosis (alkalemia) | acidosis( acidemia) |
|---|---|
| 1) increasing the PH to greater than 7/45 | 1)Lowering/reducing the PH to less than 7/35 |
| 2) increase in(blood) Carbonic Acid | 2)Reduction of (blood)Carbonic Acid |
| 3) **Reduction of/reduction in**the amount of bicarbonate ion | 3) **increasing/increase in** the amount of bicarbonate ion |
| In alkalosis we have :(severe reduction) | In Acidosis we have:(severe reduction) |
| 1) Hypo Perventilation | 1) High perventilation |
| The alkaline storage increases, too. | The alkaline storage is reduced, too. |

HCO3-base

Buffer

$\quad$ HC2O3acid

We can say it is co2 acid

H2CO4- acid

Buffer

HpO4 -2 base

H +decreases in Alkalosis: kidneys remove Hco3, but reabsorb H +

## توبول های کلیوی و تنظیم pH

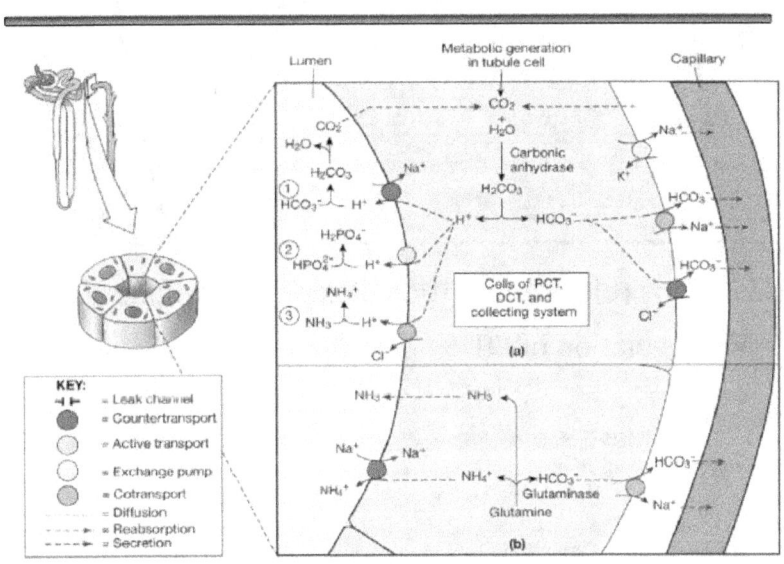

Figure 27: Kidney Tubules and pH Regulation

## توبول های کلیوی و تنظیم pH

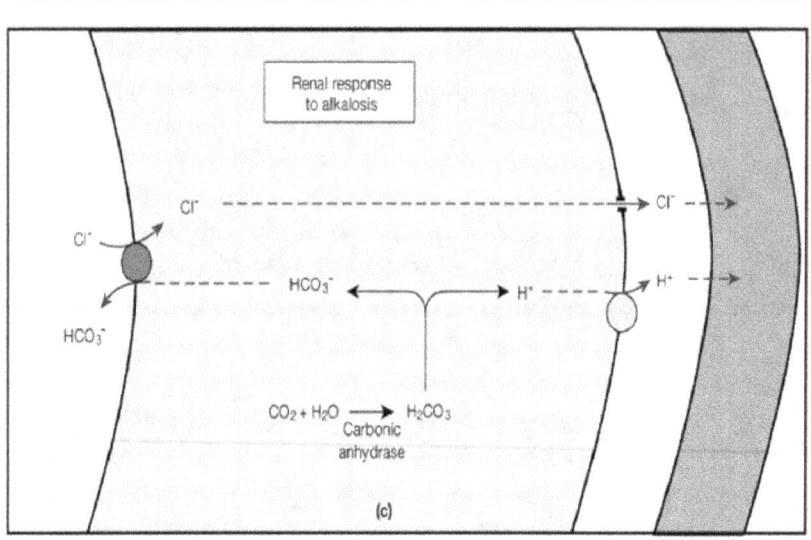

Figure 28: The role of the carbon dioxide - bicarbonate buffer system in regulation of PH

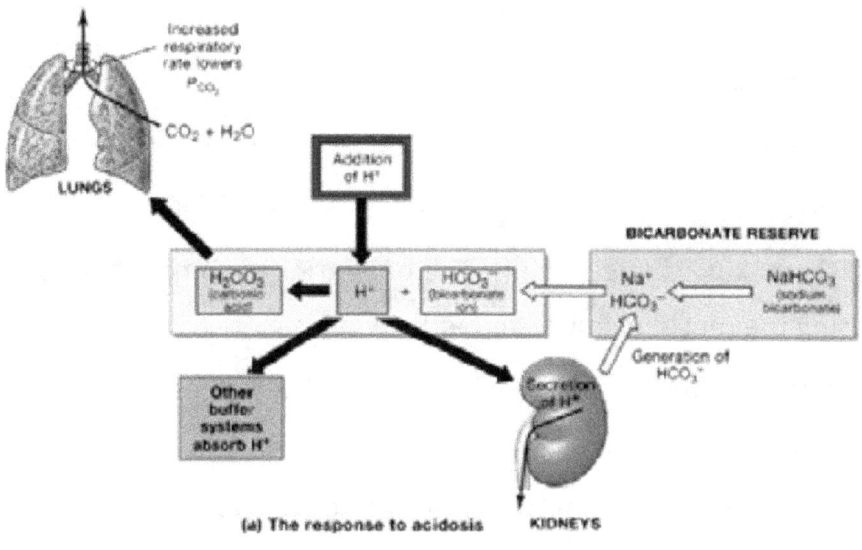

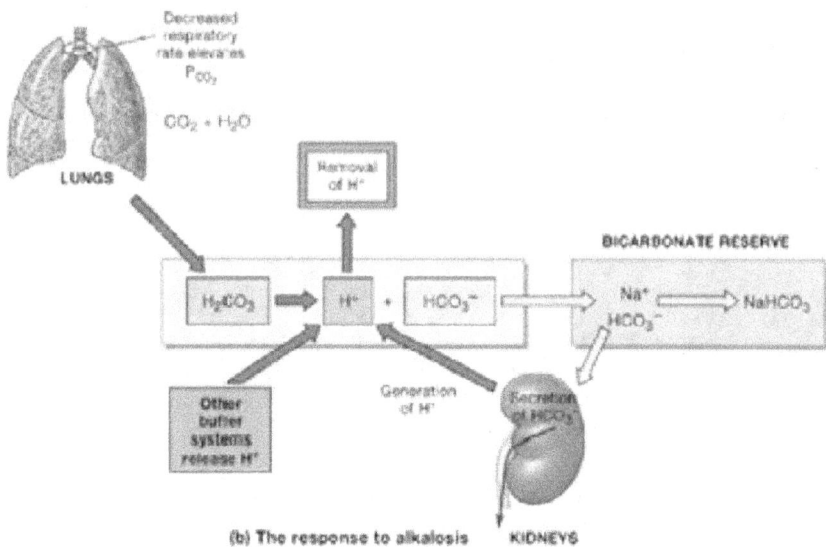

Fig.28. the role of carbon dioxide – Bicarbonate buffer system in PH-regulation

**First cause of creation acid-base disorder**

1. Metabolic: systematic changes (in cell level ).

2. Respiratory: Respiratory disorder has caused PH changes.

After making changes in pH ‹The body tries to compensate by using the mechanisms described, it will be :

1. Compensated ⟶ Normal PH ‹ The values of the components in opposite directions.

2. Relatively Compensated Both carbon dioxide and bicarbonate abnormal.

Approaching PH to normal value‹ Both carbon dioxide and bicarbonate abnormal .

3. Uncompensated ⟶ abnormal PH ‹ Only one component is abnormal.

## Hypoxia

Less than 70 years: 80- 100 mmHg

Above 70 years: 70- 100 mmHg

To reduce the O2 content of Pa called hypoxia.

**Types of Hypoxia**

1. mild: 60-80 mmHg

2. Moderate: 40- 60 mmHg

3. Sever < 40 mmHg

With a pulse oximeter to measure the oxygen content.

**Blood gas Analyser:**

The amount of oxygen and carbon dioxide are measure And testing of the ABG say.

.There are Four main types of acid-base disturbances in the body:

1. Metabolic acidosis
2. Respiratory acidosis
3. Metabolic alkalosis
4. Respiratory alkalosis

## Metabolic acidosis

Base deficit , bicarbonate (HCO3)

- PH Reduction (7/35 > )

- Decrease in plasma bicarbonate (base)

The main causes of this disorder are:

1) Increased H+ production (Lactic acidosis ،Diabetic Ketoacidosis )

2) Reduce the amount of HCO3 (Renal failure ، Diarrhea )

Ratio of 1 to 10 remain in disorder What is metabolic or renal failure.

## Compensate of disorder

In this case ، reduce of Bicarbonate or H+ increases Causing a disturbance.

Consequently, compensatory mechanisms will try to correct these two factors.

- Will step in to correct the lungs . (Hyperventilation )
- Increasing $CO_2$ removal
- thus ،$PaCO_2$ is reduced And will increase the amount of bicarbonate.

## Two compensation factors of metabolic acidosis

1) Hyperventilation (Action of the lungs)

2) Increasing $CO_2$ removal and reduce of $PaCO_2$ and Increased bicarbonate

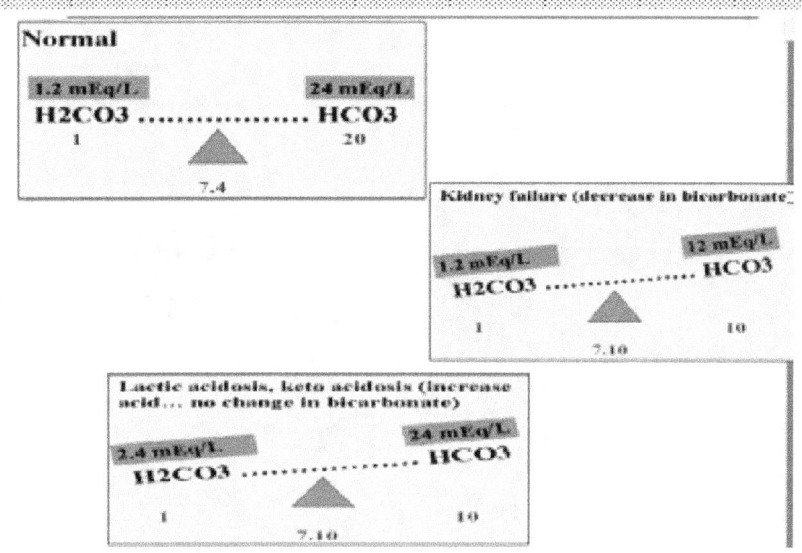

Figure 29 : Metabolic acidosis

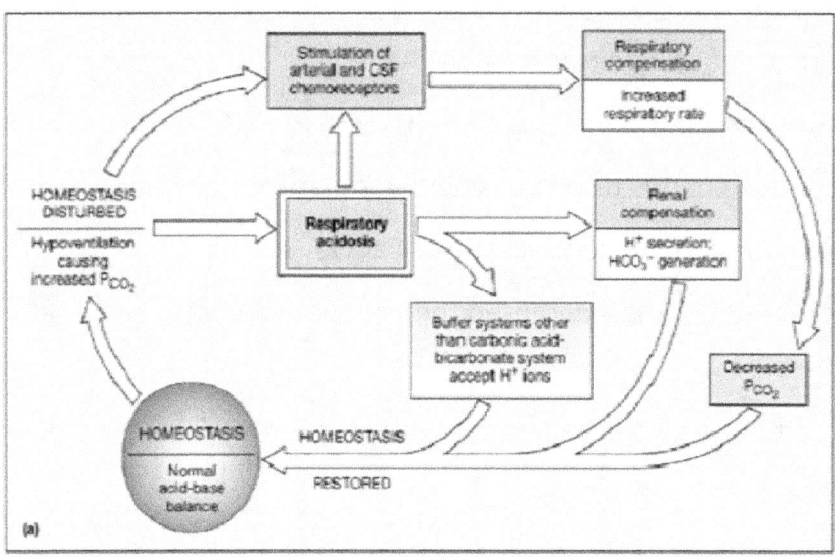

Figure 30. Respiratory regulation of acid-base

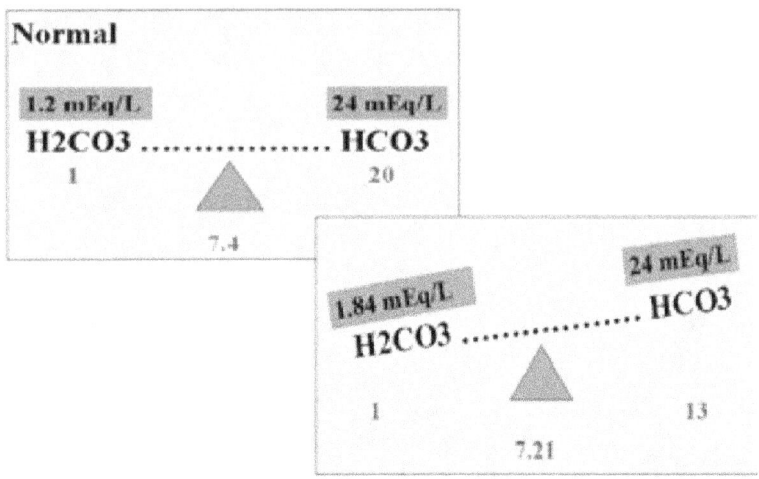

Figure 31. Respiratory acidosis

Respiratory acidosis

- increase of carbonic acid ($H_2CO_3$ )

- Reduction of $CO_2$  ↓ ← PH PH(7/35 >) ↑

- The cause of this disorder is hypoventilation.

Inhibition of expiration is creasing $PaCO_2$.

- Increased $CO_2$ has increased the production of carbonic acid in the blood.

- Breathing is high in asthma but lung function is lost.

. When $CO_2$ increases:

1) If the lungs can compensate Methylation increases.

2) if lung has a problem The kidneys attempt to compensate And renal mechanisms stimulated.

3) Buffer system

**disorder compensation**

In this case carbon dioxide increase because of breath reduction Arising from

Pulmonary disorders Causing a disturbance. Consequently, compensatory mechanisms, will try to correct the agent.

. Will step in to correct the kidneys.

. reabsorption of $HCO_3$

Reply to slowly take place.

Increasing the amount of $H_2CO_3$ reduces from Normal levels of respiratory

Acidosis.

## Metabolic alkalosis
- increase of PH (7/45 <)

- The loss of H or bicarbonate excess production causes the disorder.

The main causes of this disorder are:

1) Vomiting

2) Emptying of the stomach contents

3) Taking antacids

4) K excretion increased use of diuretics

Diuretics lowers blood pressure and may cause alkalosis.

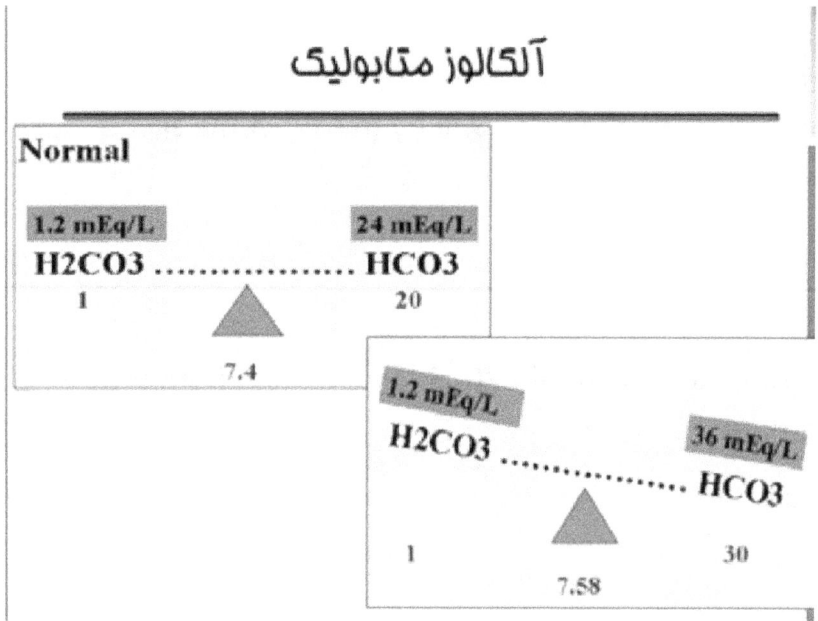

Figure 32: Metabolic alkalosis

**Compensation of disorder**

- In this case the amount of base is too much. Consequently, compensatory

Mechanisms will attempt to correct for this factor.

- Will step in to correct the lungs (Hypoventilation).

- reduce of expiratory and thereupon increased CO2.

- Thus, the pressure of PaCO2 increases and the amount of acid in the

blood will rise.


## Respiratory alkalosis
Reduction of carbonic acid (H2CO3).

- Increase in PH (7/45 < )
- This disorder is caused by hyperventilation.
- Increased exhalation, PaCO2 is reduced pressure.
- Reduction of CO2, carbonic acid reduces in blood.

Spironolactone Triggers a pump in the kidney called H+/K+ pump. Normally H+

Excretes K+ . Increased excretion of K+ catch the water and make reduction

Water of Body.


**Compensate of disorder**

In this case reduction of carbon dioxide due to increase of Increased breathing

Caused by Pulmonary Disorder caused disturbance.

Consequently, compensatory

mechanisms will try to correct for this factor. Will step in to correct the kidneys.

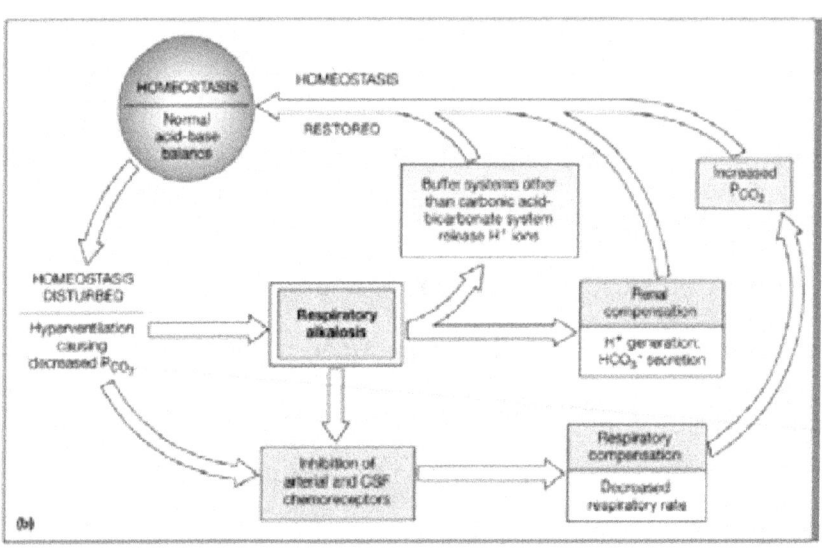

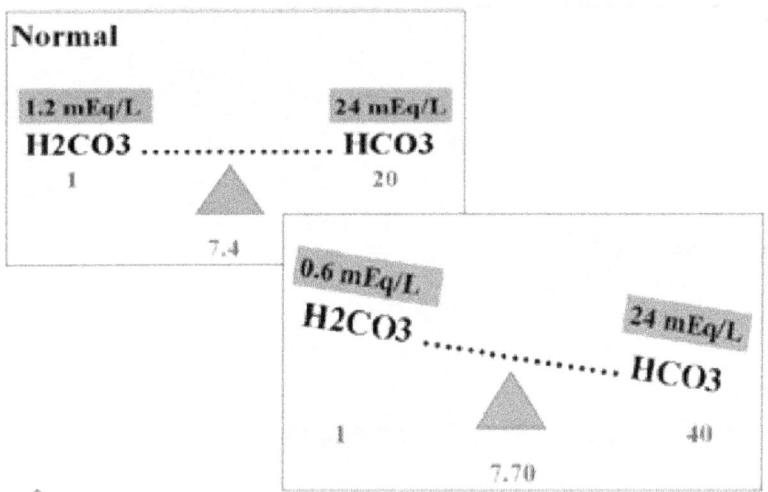

Figure 33. Respiratory alkalosis

ABg: They heparinized syringe and draw the femoral artery. Done on arterial

Blood gases Because of interactions with cells.

. Anticoagulants: Sodium citrate, Heparin, EDTA.

Of each type of anticoagulant can not be used for any type of test. EDTA used

For counting. If they heparinized, blue stained all the cells.

$PH = 7.4 \pm 0.05$

$PaCO_2 = 35$ mmHg

$HCO_3^- = 24$ mEq

(Alkalosis) Respiratory acidosis $PaCO_2 \uparrow\downarrow \rightarrow CO_2 \uparrow\downarrow \rightarrow H_2CO_3$

$PaCO_2 \uparrow\downarrow \rightarrow PH \uparrow\downarrow \rightarrow$ (Acidosis) alkalosis $PaCO_2 \propto \dfrac{1}{PH}$

$HCO_3^- \uparrow\downarrow$ (Alkalosis) metabolic acid

1) In the first case: In the first case: lung problems, kidney did not compensate.

2) partially compensated because PH is not returned to normal.

3) In the third case: that compensated Because PH is returned to normal.

PHα Compensation occurred, Return to normal.

The problem of the kidney = $HCO_3^-$ α Metabolic

The problem of pulmonary = $CO_2$ α Respiratory

Question: PH = 7.3, PaCO2 = 24 , HCO3⁻?

Acidosis and respiratory alkalosis are mixed.

## Electrolytes and minerals:

. Sodium: PR is not binding for sodium and sodium-free in the blood.

- The most basic electrolyte of the body.
- The determinate osmolality of the extracellular fluid volume and balance of
the body
- The normal concentration of that is 136-145 meq/L .
- The most important role of that is in The function of muscles and nerves.
- Sodium Disorders

. Hyponatremia: Plasma sodium decreased to less than 125meg/L.

. hypernatremia: Increase in serum sodium over 145 meg / L

- Some ions in the cytosol and some are out of the cytosol.
- Total $Ca^{2+}$ concentration is low. Cells always lowers $Ca^{2+}$ levels .
- $Ca^{2+}$ is bound to albumin in the blood and bounds to calmodulin and Calbindin

In the cell.

. Calcium is stored in mitochondria.

- $Mg^{2+}$: Inside the cell is more than outside the cell.

. kinases that deal with ATP need the $Mg^{2+}$ and carbohydrate metabolism pathway

also requires magnesium.

- Chloride is the major extracellular anion.

. The chlorine pump to be pulled into the cell and carbon dioxide is removed and

The pump is called band (3) where is in the RBC and Carbon dioxide is produced by

the carbonic anhydrase with help the Zn.

*** Calbindin is a protein that that binds to calcium in the intestine.that active

By help vitamin D.

Calcium binding to troponin C in muscle .

. calmodulin is binding to Ca in muscles.

## Potassium

- main Cation of intracellular

- Creation of cell membrane potential with potassium exit from the cell.

- Regulation of intracellular ions and fluid balance
- PH Balance

## Potassium disorders

1) Hypokalemia

- Plasma potassium decreased to less than 3/5 mg/l
- in this case The loss of magnesium , phosphorus and calcium are also seen .
- Under the influence of insulin, Extracellular potassium into cells is inserted.
- Alkalosis: Substitution of extracellular potassium and intracellular hydrogen

And K+ excretion instead of H+ from the kidneys to compensate for the alkaline

Conditions.


2) Hyperkalemia

- Plasma potassium decreased to less than 5mg/l

## Chlorine

- The major extracellular anion
- Red blood cells in the blood of their role in buffering stages replace their chloride

With bicarbonate ion .

## Calcium

- The most abundant body mineral

- Enzymes activity, hormonal response, blood clotting, muscle contraction.

- signal transduction in place synapses

- the normal concentration in the body is 8/5-10 mg/l.

## The role of calcium in the blood coagulation

There are A series of factors. Vitamin K is involved in blood clotting that activates

Four of the coagulation system. Factor of 2, 7, 9 and 10.

2) by help of heat carboxylation (Vitamin K) to these factors in the gamma

Part of factors COO- on the wall of a blood vessel caused and there is also

Ca+, Platelets are also causing sticking together and clotting occurs.

## Magnesium

- Major intracellular cation.

- it has role of cofactor for many enzymes.

- Transmission of nerve – muscle.

## Magnesium deficiency

- Alcoholism, diuretics and metabolic acidosis.

**Symptoms of deficiency:** Weakness of muscle tremors and heart arrhythmias.

. Magnesium supplements to prevent calcium oxalate stone formation, and also

Lowers blood pressure.

## Cachexia : Overweight

lipid serum (Like choline) And give glucose serum to the cancers and give Mg+

too:

1) Fall in blood pressure.
2) Nutrient uptake increases as the vessel does not transmit .
3) Metabolism

## Phosphate

- 85% in muscle and 15% in other tissues.
- Only there is 1% in the extracellular space.
- Metabolic and structural actions.

**Phosphate deficiency**

- The reduction of consumption, increase in Excretion ( hyperparathyroidism)

And translocation into the cell (Taking insulin).

- the most important molecule the has Phosphate is ATP. nucleic acids have

Also Phosphate.

**Zinc**

- in many structure of metalloenzymes is involves.

- Carbonic Anhydrase, Alkaline phosphatase, RNA and DNA Polymerase.

- The structure of the zinc finger DNA binding protein plays a role.

- there is in Gostyn ( salivary polypeptides ).

- In the normal development of taste buds is involved.

- for Cytokine production is required.

- there is in structure of Porphobilinogen synthase.

- Zinc deficiency: Incomplete growth and sexual development disorder,

Poor wound healing, Dermatitis, Loss of taste, Immune Dysfunction, Anemia.

. Zinc finger is a motif that Based on DNA and responds to steroid hormones.

. they act in The sprouts of hair, skin and epithelial cells and cell sex, RNA and

DNA polymerase that DNA and RNA don't act if zinc If zinc does not work and

These cells are difficult.

For example, germ cells is impaired, infertility and the skin will heal wounds later.

. Some anemias, such as Pernicious anemia due to Zinc and iron deficiency.

Immune disorder ⟶ Cytokine

Anemia ⟶ Synthesis of haem

**Haem**

- There is in the structure of the haem proteins.

- Hemoglobin, myoglobin, catalase, peroxidase and cytochromes

Transfer by transferrin and stored by Ferritin and Hemosiderin

**Haem deficiency**

.Excretion of haem - containing cells (Bleeding or loss of epithelial cells)

- hemochromatosis: Accumulation of haem in tissues (desferal or desferrioxamine

Used to treat patients with hemochromatosis.

Haem Pr → Cytochrome C and Chlorophyll

⟶ The body is not excreted haem, Unless forced such as bleeding. Haem in

intestinal cells (Beginning of the small intestine) to be stored for two days,

otherwise the cell is dug, enter stool and outs.

Calcification: a decrease lysyl oxidase oxidase in bone is involved.

Copper

- Is participating in structure of Metalloproteinase proteins .

- Cytochrome oxidase, superoxide dismutase, ferroxidase, Ceruloplasmin,

Lyzyl oxidase, Dopamine hydroxylase, $\Delta 9 - C18$ Desaturase.

- Transport in the blood through albumin, in Tissues is binding to Ceruloplasmin.

. Copper deficiency symptoms : Anemia, Hypercholesterolemia, not Mineralization

Of bone, Leukopenia, Thin large arteries and lack of Neural tissue Demyelinated.

- Zinc (Zn) increases caused Copper uptake impaired.

**Menkes syndrome:** Decrease of copper absorption (The main symptoms of

this syndrome, is curly hair)

**Wilson's disease:** Increase in deposition of copper in the tissues , particularly the

Liver.

- Treatment with chelating agents, such as penicillin

**Who has Copper deficiency :**

- has anemia (Copper also plays a role in the synthesis)

- Ceruloplasmin helps in intestinal haem absorption, if copper is absent, the

Ceruloplasmin is also absent, so haem is not absorbed.

## Chrome

A part of chromodulin That facilitate insulin binding to its receptor. (GTF a

complex of chromium, nicotinic acid and several amino acids.

**Chrome deficiency:** Impaired glucose transport.

- Diabetes leads to increased urinary excretion of chromium .

. The insulin receptor is a tyrosine oxidase .

. Some diabetes is due to chromium deficiency .

## Selenium

- With vitamin E are including antioxidants in the body.

- it participate in structure of Glutathione peroxidase and iodothyronine

Deiodinase.

. Selenium is an antioxidant .

. Glutathione peroxidase : reduction the Glutathione oxidized, detoxifies and

For practice, selenium is required.

. iodothyronine Deiodinase: there is in thyroid and tissues, Causes T 4 conversion

to T3 (In peripheral tissues), T-4 is a prohormone and And T-3 do all the works.

# Chapter 3

## Carbohydrates disorders

People to provide their ATP needs to be consumed daily 120 g of glucose.

- Tissue lacking mitochondria or mitochondrial less, exclusively on glycolysis for

Use energy.

- RBC, The cornea, lens and part of retina.

- The inner part of the kidney, Testicles, Leukocytes, And white muscle fibers

- these tissues consume only 40 g of glucose daily.

- Glucose as an energy source for cells in the intestinal wall could be considered,

However, these cells can provide more energy from glutamine catabolism.

. Glucose is absorbed through the veins moves to the liver.

- The liver is the first organ that is located after the pancreas .

- Exposed to the highest concentration of insulin and glucagon.

. The mitochondria in red blood cells is low So, glycolysis is needed. glucose

is absorbed into the portal vein and into the liver (vien both into the liver and outs)( In glomerular artery enters and exits)

## Digestion and absorption of carbohydrates in the body

- D-Glu is the main fuel of most organisms and Plays major role in the metabolism.

- Many carbohydrates other than glucose after becoming a combination of

intermediates enter this pathway.

- The most important carbohydrates that are consumed by humans:

. Polysaccharides: starch and glycogen

. Disaccharides: maltose, lactose, trehalose and sucrose

. Monosaccharides: fructose, mannose and galactose

. Each sugar intake and has metabolism, enter the glucose pathway.

Hexokinase effects on three Carbohydrates:

1) Fruct**ose**

2) Mannose

3) Glucose

. Fructokinase is in the liver makes Fructose-1-phosphate.

. Aldolase has 3 isozyme (Have the same performance)

. Aldolase B is in the liver cells and toxic, if accumulates in the cell, Liver catch

hereditary fructose intolerance.

. Aldolase (a) is in the muscle Its deficiency causes Duchenne muscular syndrome

And there is a lack of energy.

. aldolase C is in most tissues.

. the glottis is Glucose transporters to the cell.

. Glottis ( 1 ) says the erythrocyte. brain Glottis.

. Glottis ( 2 ) is independent of the rate, Meaning The higher the glucose level is low

That works (Liver, liver cells , liver) .

. Glottis ( 3 ) is the glottis brain. Neuron-specific

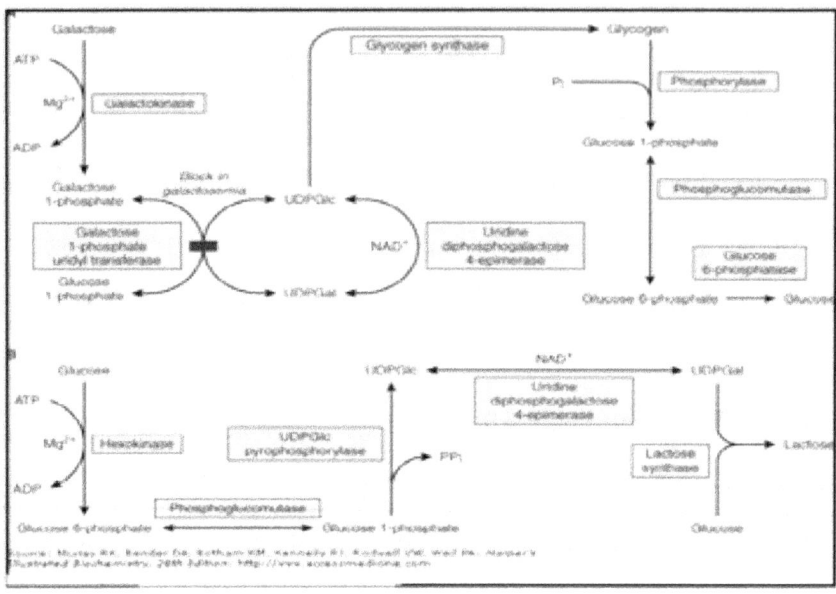
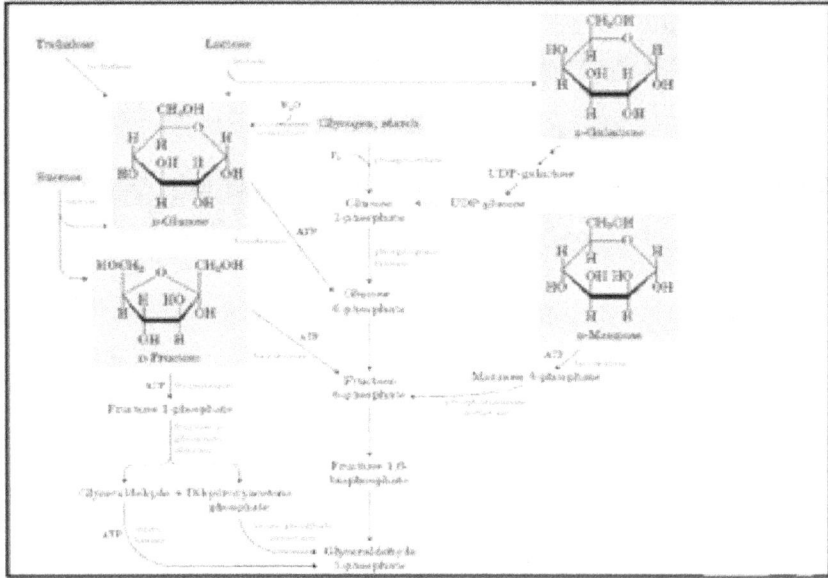

Figure 34. cycles of Glycogenolysis and Glycogenesis and Galactose and glycolysis

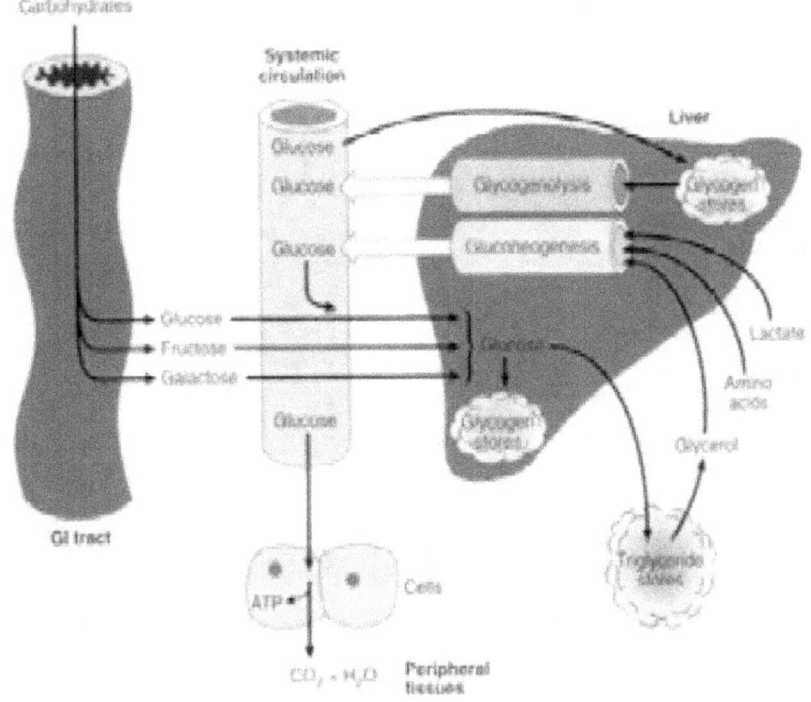

Figure 35. Glucose homeostasis

. Glottis 4 is in muscle and adipose tissue, there is after the meal and increase of sugar.

. Glottis 5 is the fructose transporter. does not transmit the glucose.

. Glottis 7 is in microsomes (Endoplasmic reticulum), especially in the liver. transmissions

The glucose from the network to out.

. structure of glottis 6 is varies with other glottis. Because first time transmits

The glucose is classified in The glottis.

The difference

1) In various tissues

2) Action

3) Effect and dependence of hormone

4) affinity

. Somatostatin: plays Stimulation GH secretion.
Pancreaticobiliary polypeptide

Is component of exocrine pancreatic material.

. The effect of glucagon on adipose tissue to produce FFA. The mechanism of

Glucagon effect with protein

. Chains A and B are connected by two disulfide connectivity And a disulfide

Bonding is in the chain a.

. Insulin is secreted as Perry prohormones.

. Insulin is the primary structure, Because neither alpha helix and beta sheet.

. Glucose by the glottis 2 enters the pancreas.

. ATP production of insulin secretion :

1) Is inhibited the K+ pump

2) Causing activates the Na-K/ATPase.

3) With production of CAMP causes the release of calcium from cellular Stores.

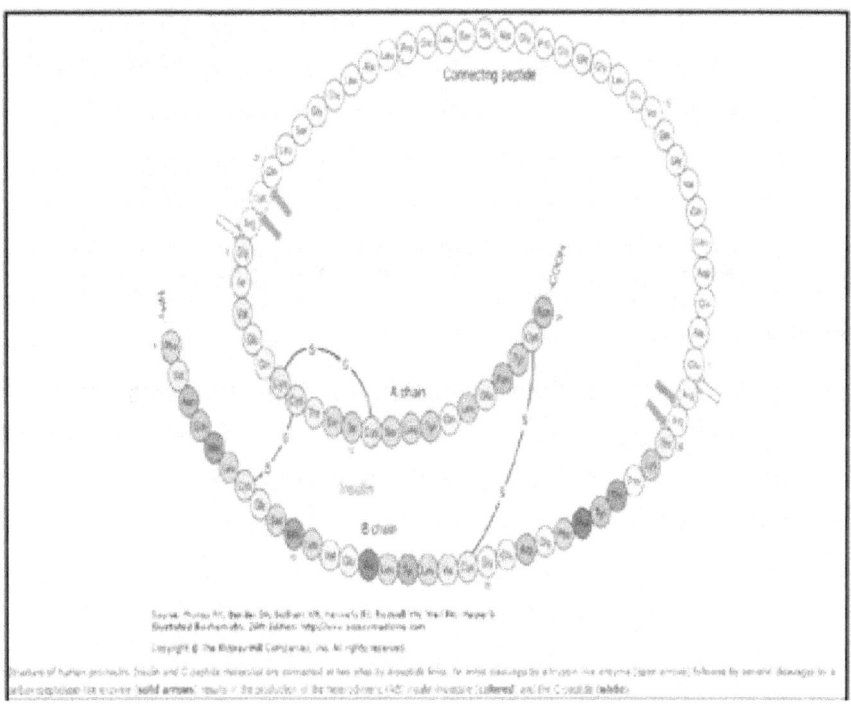

Figure 36. Disulfide bonds and And A and B chains of insulin.

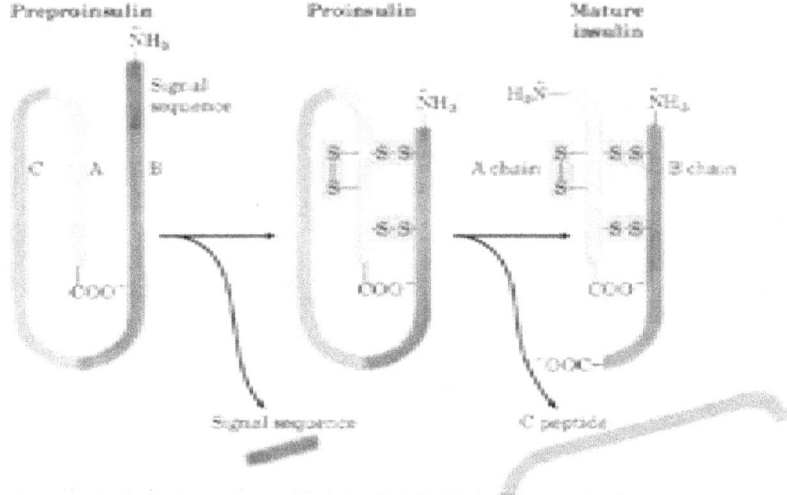

Figure 37. Perry prohormones and prohormones and Mature insulin. Signal-s

leading Insulin is guided into vesicles and stored. C peptide removes the insulin

and causes mature insulin.

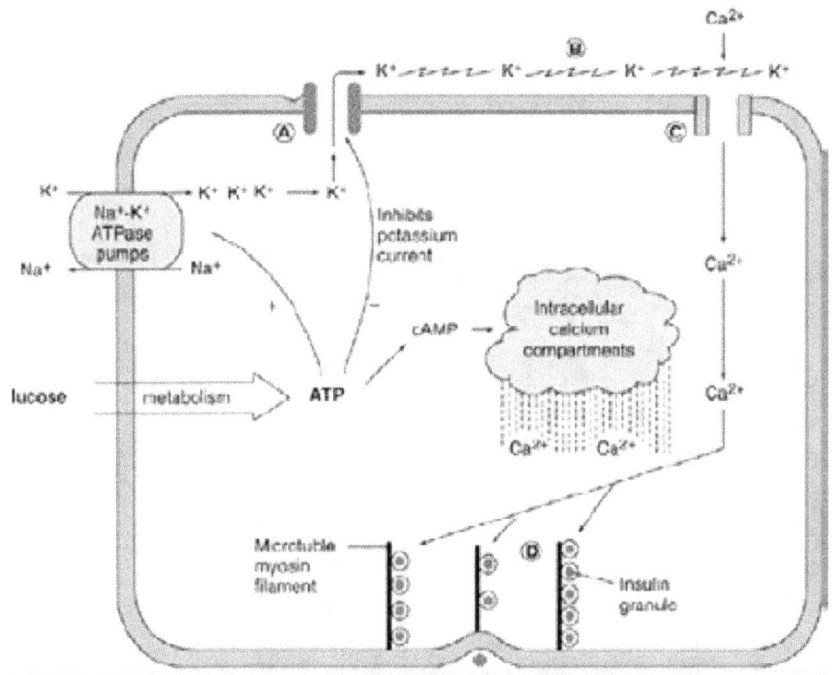

Figure 38. The mechanism of insulin secretion

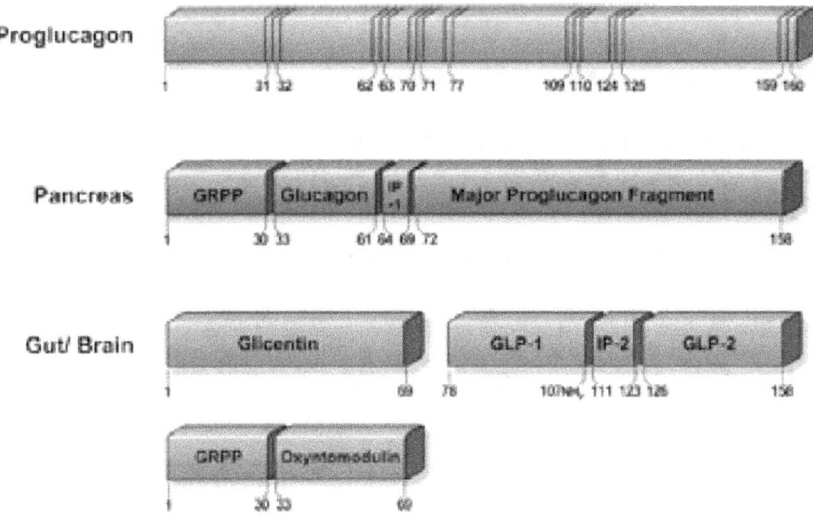

Figure 39. Various forms of glucagon in different organs

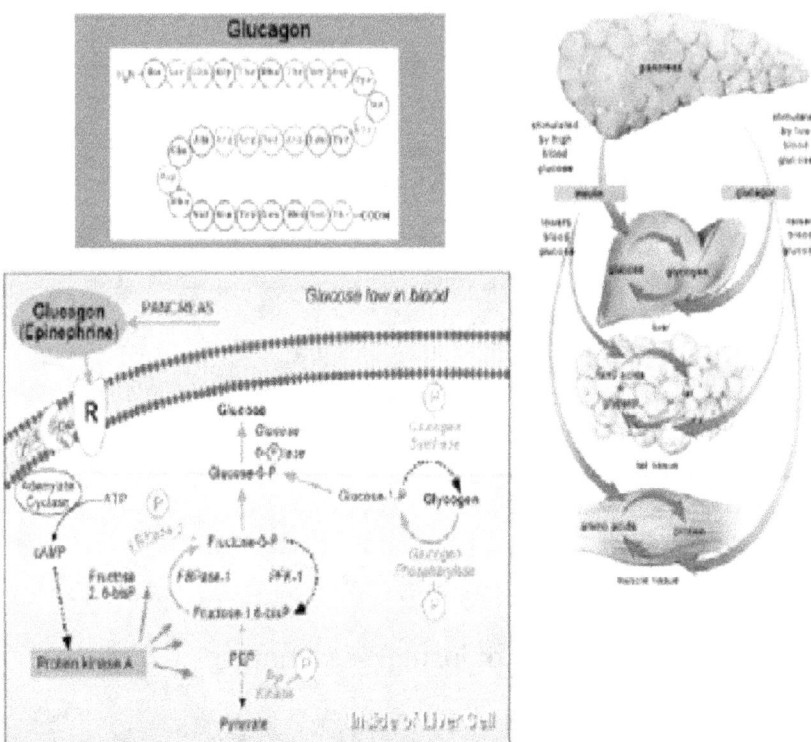

Figure 40. The mechanism of action of glucagon.

⟶ K+ is normally pumped out of the cell and inhibit Ca2+ pumps.

⟶ ATP inhibits the potassium pump and The potassium inside the cell increases

And leads to the activation of Na+ and K+ and Na increases out of the cell .

Membrane depolarizes and Membrane depolarization causes activation of the Ca2+

Pump (Voltage-dependent). Calcium into the cell, and calcium increases.

Increased energy By the action of adenylate cyclase converts to CAMP.

CAMP effects on ca2+ deposits leading to increase of Ca2+ Whatever way

insulin acts to reduce blood glucose levels .

World Diabetes Day :::14 nowember

World Diabetes Epidemic: 2003-2005 (Million people)

2003= 194 million

2025= 333 million

the largest epidemic in the world, is diabetes.

The number of people with diabetes show in the figure.

major cause of type 2 diabetes is Obesity.

Universal,global

14 th November is universal day of Diabetes

Diabetes universal Epidemi : 2003-2025

(million personal)

In year 2003, we had 194 millions of diabetiesperson.In year 2025 we will have 333 millions ofdiabetiesperson.Diabet, now is the most Epidemi in the world. Fatness is main reason of type II diabet.

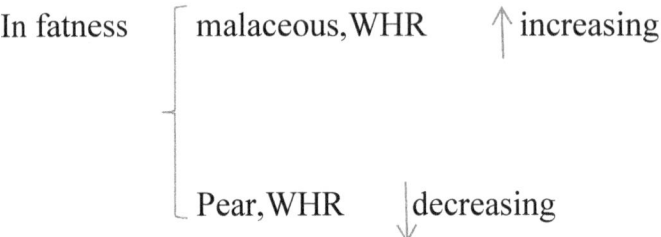

In fatness
- malaceous, WHR ↑ increasing
- Pear, WHR ↓ decreasing

One kind of Epidemi is Diabet : Due to statics of Who in year 2000,171 million persons had been suffering to diabet. (2.8% in world population). And probably in year 2030 this amount will be twice.

Complications of diabetes are the main reason for death and direction diseases.(In year 2002).

Patients :

90% of diabeties patients cure with medical primary controls.

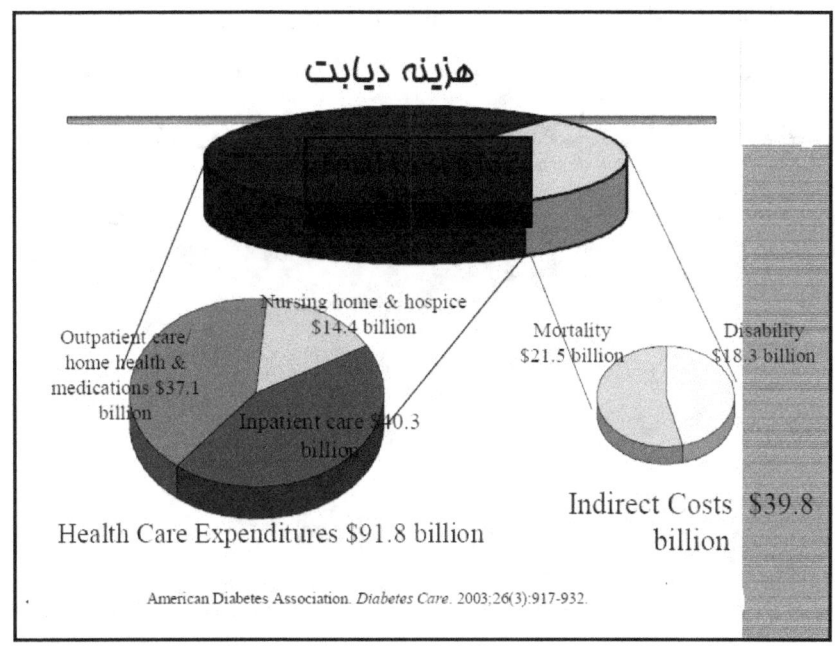

Figure 41: Diabet'S cost

Figure 42: Blood Glucose after using Glucose in Normal and Diabetic curnes :

گلوکز خون پس از مصرف گلوکز در افراد سالم و دیابتیک

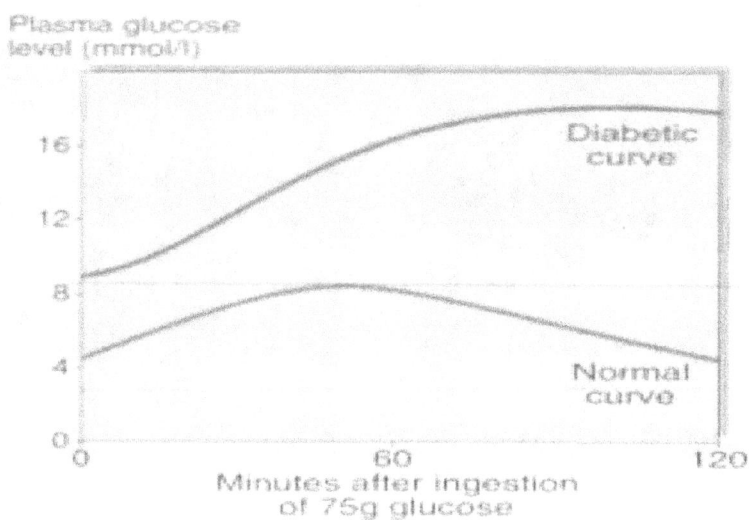

**Diabets types:**

1. Diabetes type I  ⟶ Dimolition B cell
2. Diabetes type II  ⟶ Advancer deficiency in Insulin excretion.

3० other diabetes typiesGenetic deficiency in B celles action
　　　　　　　　　　Insulin activity
　　　　　　　　　　Pancreas exocrine disease
　　　　　　　　　　Diabetes as the result of chemical materials or Drugs.
4० Diabetes mellitus of pregnancy period.


Metabolic Disruption :

DKA : In this condition amount of blood ketoacidesdecreas. It is specific for type I diabetes. In this type of diabetes B-cell dimolitiedm non-apperance of Insuline,Blood sugar swelled but the body refusal it so appeal to futtly acids, KBs increased and Oxidize,$H^+$ improve, PH decrease and diabetes acidose forms.

HONK : It is specific for Type II diabetes. In this type of diabetes the celles resists to Insulin and reply to insulin diminishe.Blood sugar improve.Insulinsecreted,make an impression on liver obstacle from acidose and exeretion of KBs.

What is the reason of Hyperosmoullar? White Both sugar and water secreted from urine, amount of water diminish but sugar remain in blood,so hyper osmoullar established.

Coma : sugar do not be able to inter to the sugar cell there forefollowing points results :

1.While B hidroxyButiric acid do not produc so brain do not receive Energy.

2.Since amount of water decreases,blood pressure diminishe then amount of electrolits changes.

Glucose Analysis methods :

1.Hexokyanize

2.Glucose oxidase

3. Glucose dehudrogenaseMethodes for Glucose measuring :

1.Anzymatic courses 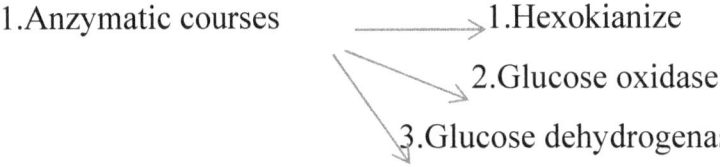 1.Hexokianize

2.Glucose oxidase

3.Glucose dehydrogenase

2.Chemical courses ⟶ orthotoloiedyn

Sugars with annelideAmins compounds exposed to Acidacetic and temperature produces a base shiff. Wich is in Hexoses, green colour and in pentoses orange colour.

Because orthotoloiedyn is cancergenesis and destrogs the laboratory materials and facilities so use no more of that.

## GlucosilarHomoglobin(HbA1c):

-contiyuity of Glucose to final chain amins group cause to form HbA1c.

-HbA1c concentration depends on blood Glucose concentration and incresead time.

-Due to amount of HbA1c that measures with chromatography,shows blood sugar concentration in 6 or 8 past week.

-In proof of cure effectiving, we can use from glucosilarHomoglobin concentration changes in diabetes patients.

-Total Homoglobin in Normal persones is less than 5.7%

-Glucose connected to type c and glucosilar.

-Both HbA1c and diabetes are connected.

-HbA1c is for cure pre manentation, not for distinction.

In Diabetes patients:

-Total Homoglobin less than 5.7%  ⟶ strong control

-Total Homoglobin between 5.7 - 6.4%  ⟶ unreliable control.

-Total Homoglobin more than 6.5%  ⟶ poor control.

HbA1c has several types.mention them?

## Diabetes Distinction Standards : (criterions):

1. If for first time, BG(blood sugar) is more than 200 mg/dl so person has diabetes.

2. fasting FBC mesearing.

3. pregnancy Diabetes mesearing $\longrightarrow$ OGTT = 2 hpp = 2 hour post pravial

- forweman that did not had Diabetes, GDM riddling doing with OGTT test in middle of 24-28 weeks of pregnancy.

- OGTT test is for pregnancy (distinction).

- GDM test is for pregnancy diabetes distination.

FBC $\longrightarrow$ 92 mg/dl (8.5 mmol/L)

Lh $\longrightarrow$ 180 mg/dl (10.0 mmol/L)

2h $\longrightarrow$ 153 mg/dl (8.5 mmol/L)

- pregnancy diabetes test doing in tree final mounth.

## 2-hpp test :

- false increase $\longrightarrow$ eclipsed of Nicotine and caffeine.

- false decrease $\longrightarrow$ Because of Acetaminophen and oxycodone in recognition of using glucose oxidase method.

- Stress inexpert of Acute diseases, infection, pregnancy and surgery establishes unreliable result.

- In this test Glucose unnormal decreasing confirms with OGTT test.

Glu $\underline{\quad\text{Pink colour}\quad}$ Within termogen $\longrightarrow$

OGTT is for test confirmation $\longrightarrow$ The patient

Must uses 150gr glucose and 300 ml,75-100 gr in 3days Latter if he/she could not eat them we must accomplish IGTT test.

In this method first accomplish FBS, if it was high (more than 350) it is critical do not carrg out OGTT test again.

Distinction between GCT and OGTT :

1. In GCT used from 50 gr sugar.

2. In GCT dial not need to eating 150 gr glucose in 3 days.

GCT $\longrightarrow$ GDM

In OGTT test :

- In 30,60,90,120 minutes after eating glucose a complish blood test.

If used from 100gr glucose, must a ccomplish blood test, 3 hours later.

- ACOG a ccomplished in pregnancy test. Which test using 75 gr and which test using 100gr glucose?

ACOG Test $\longrightarrow$ 100gr glucose

ADA Test $\longrightarrow$ 75gr glucose

Distinction between Type I and II Diabetes :

- patients which have type I diabetes,they find an expression like as cashecsy.

In type I,body weight is low (In type II it is high) 10% patients have types I.

Connection to genetics type I is less than type II.

In type I B-cell had diminished and resistence to insulin exists. In Type II in final processes insulin will be decreased. In type I patients have must to use insulin for cure (probsbly in type II patients did not need to using insulin never and it is curable with a simple nourishing)

Imagin an Auto-immani disease and shows disease revolation by means of syllogism?

An viral infection with genetic deficiency enter to body,so Abs forms antagonist of B-cells, after so many times, Abs amount improved and diminished B-cells,at the end we will have no more of cell.

Why insulin in type II diabetes first increased,then decreased?

At the first we have genetics deficiency in B-cells receptor; factors like as fatness, age addition and life's manner are stimulatore.the other normal factor secreted and improve resistance insuline :

Glucose increased and forced the cell to secreted more insuline,so cell ability is limited; glucose increase is harmful for cell so cell diminished,insulin decreased and body needs to insulin injection.

In primary courses of this type of diabetes, must changesd the life's manner but at the end insulin injected.

Type II Diabetes progress :

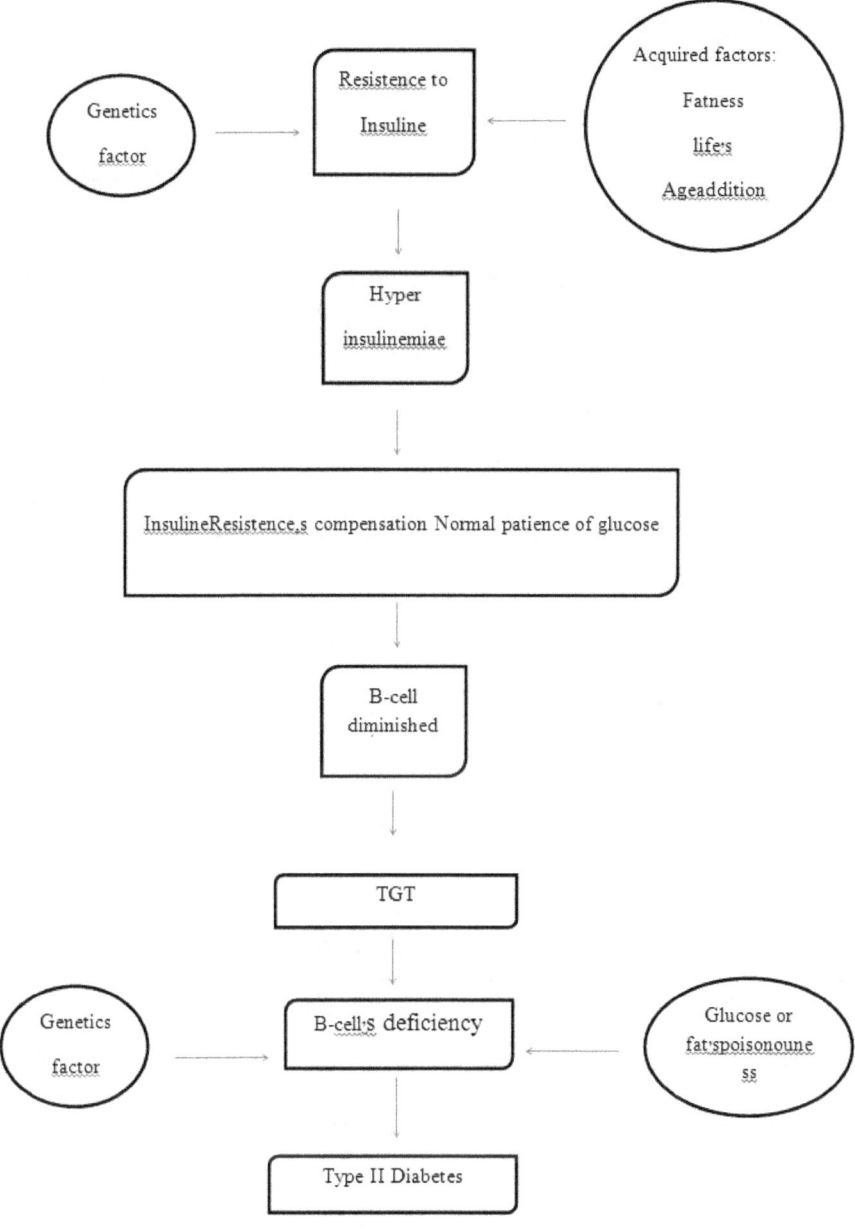

Figure 43 : Type II Diabetes progress

Insuline Resistance importance :

90% Type II diabetes patience have insulin Resistance.

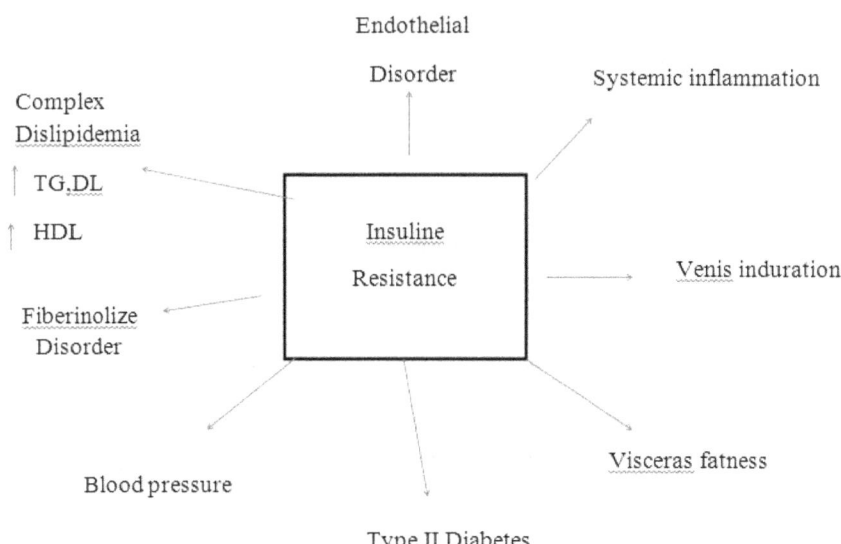

Figure 44 :Insulineresistunce importance

Diabetes Problems:

| Macrovascular vessels | Microvascular vessels |
|---|---|
| Circumferential vessels diabetese | Diabetes Retinopathy |
| Coronare vessels disease | Diabetes Nephropathy |
| Brain vessels disease | Diabetes Nephropathy |

Schedule 17 : Diabetes problems Microvascular taxes have spare connection with HbA1s and blood sugar 's amount and macrovascular problems have connection with sugar increased time.

High amount of glucose resulting

Following characteristic :

1. Diabetes foot

2. Cataract

3. Cutaneous problems

4. Infection

5. Glucorna

After type II diabetes distination, at first we must study microvascular problems in patience.

Tow kinds of complication :

1. microvascular : It is instantaneous in small vessels (confirmer)

2. macrovascular : It is gradual in large vessels (venous) (vessels or unvessels)

⟶ (Depositing In venous mitrals) ⟶ resulting stroke.

Due to molecular knowledge while Hyperglycemia happens some metabolics characteristic and pathway actives :

1. proteikinasec

2. glycation

3. polyol pathway

These factors accomplished to an phenomenon which names ((micro Angiopathy)).

Why pkc have been activated in Hyperglycemia?

Mechanism:

When polyol activated ⟶ Sorbitol pathway flun activated and increased.

When Glycation activatedAGEP increased.

When protein kinasec activated    Amount of cell'sphosphorylation,sugar and HexoesAmins have been increased.

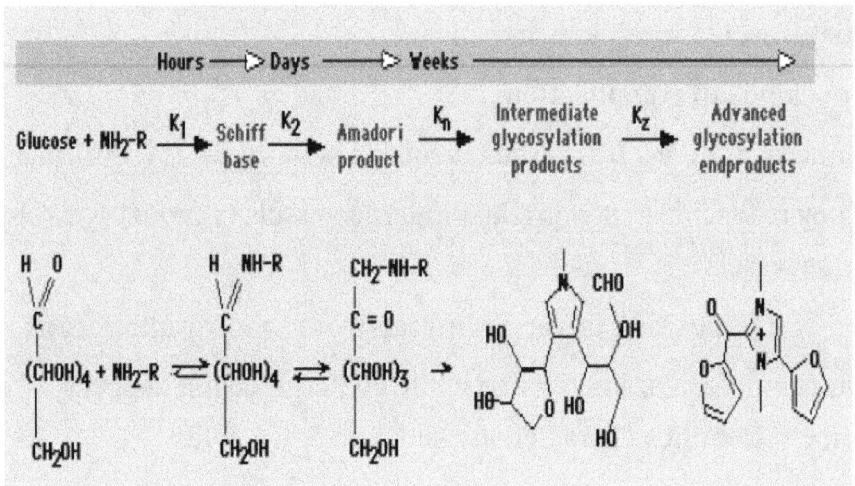

Figure 45 : AGEP formation

What is AGEP? Define the meaning of AGEP?

-Advanced Glycation Ending products names AGEP.

-Increasing of matter amount is one of the factors.

Which improves the reaction speed. Matterials reaction probability rises when glu increased. Protein is the most dangerous matter which reaction whit glu,thenglu reaction with amine band creates one base-shiff that changes protein syllogism.one week until one year after these reactions, Agepcreateds which eclipsed of protein has been changed. If protein be inner the cell will be unactivate even though be in surface of the cell introduces the cell like as friegn matter.

Drugs are studing now for AGEP,s prevention.

There is an disease in one of the diabetes type that names A canthosisNigricans which creates brown spots on the neekskin.consider it?

Hypoglaicimia :

Blood sugar decreasing symptom :

1.perspire

2.vertigo

3.tremor

4.weariness

5.hunger

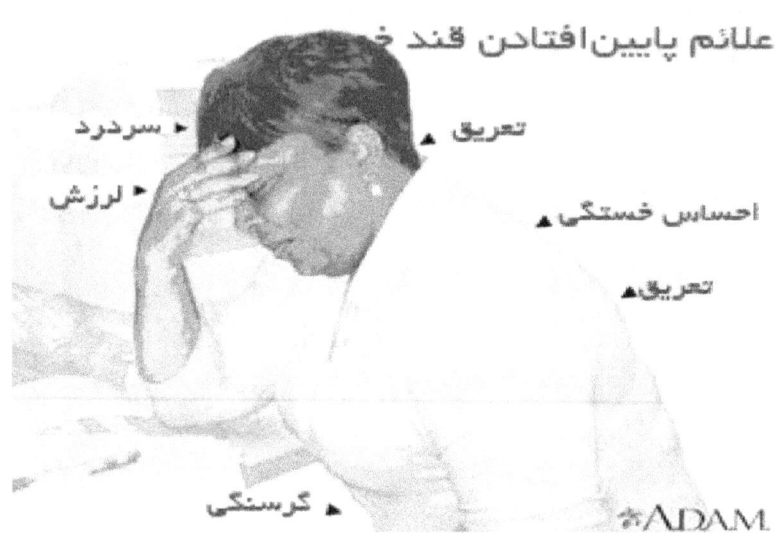

Figure 46 :Hypoylaicimia symptoms

Hypoylaicimia types separating :

-patient has hypoylaicimia,if sugar be less than 65.

-There is two test for considering Hypoylaicimia after distinction.

1.Insuline test

2.C-peptid test

If amount of both Insuline and c-peptid was low ↓ the causes could be alcohol,drugsAcut state of malaria disease and etc.

Because of entering insulin from out of thebody,c-peptid increased and insulin decreased.(Insuline Normal state both of them;Insuline and c-peptid; secreted with together and their amount is similar.)

Both, insulin and c-peptid,were high.(the cell secreted too much).

In Ansulinemiadiseas which curse with sulphonylureas that affected on insulin secreted and there is B-cell tumore.

**Carbohydraties metabolism disease:**

1.(MODY) happens.Because of below characterizes:

-Melintuth Diabetes type II

-GlucokinaseDificiency

2.Because of below characterizes,hcrediatary fructose intolerance happens:

-B-AldolaseDificiency

-fructose-1-phosphate gathering and Both pi, ATP decreasing in liver.

Cell diminished because of dependent ATP pumps disabling.

An special form of type II diabetes which happens because of glucokinase deficiency names Mody.

Fructose orotic : Because of fructokainase deficiency, fructose repluse increase in urea and Gl symptom decrease.

3.Below items creates,homolatic Anemia :

-Pirrovatkainase deficiency

-ATP deficiency specialy for Na-k ATpase pump activity in adult RBC.

-Reticolusites,normal ranges of ATP

4. Below items creates fructoserotic:

-fructokainase deficiency

-fructose gathering in blood and urine.

-cell diminished because of dependent ATP pumps diablling.

RBCs did not have mitoconria,just have glyculization which is half-alone and names shentramman. Glycerat-2-kinase enzyme which changes 1,3- BisphosphoGlycerate to 3-phospho Glyceratprouducees one ATP in this reaction .pirrovat kinase produces one ATP too.so there are 4-ATP.that two numbers of it uses and two remains for RBC.

There is one shent that change 1,3-diphospho glyscrate to 2,3-Diphosphogli serate eclipsed of mutaseenzyme then 2,3 phosphoglyserat eclipsed of phosphatase changes to 3-phosphoGlycerat which uses one ATP in this reaction.

BPG connected between two Homoglobin B-chain,It has any affected on $o_2$ connection in lung but drops $o_2$ in tissues.then connected to T form so oxygene dropped easily.

RBC founds like as T form in tissues and it founds like as R form in lung.

In some person because of pirrovatekainase enzyme (which produces ATP) deficiency,RBCinvoied deficiency too and disabled. There for water homeostasis changes, the cell diminished,RBC decrease and hemolysis anemia creates(becase of RBC lysis ) but Reticulocytes (RBCs) remains Normal because they have others pathway for producing energy inaddition to glycolysis.

Homoglubin because of conformationg changing from R to T form,cantak $o_2$ in lung and dropsin tissues.

5.Because of below items,pirrovatedehydrogenasis complex Dificiency happens:

-Lactate,pirrovate , Alanin increasing.

-Lacticacidosis

It has like as pirrovatdohydrogenasis kinase inhibitor in body chlocholoroacetate cure.

6.Favism happens because of below items :

-Glucose G-phosphatdehydrogenasis deficiency.

-Decreasing of needed NADPH for glution reducing.

-Reticulocyte increasing

7.Glactusomia Including below items :

-Gulactose 1-phosphate uridiltransferase deficiency and Gulactokainasemilad deficiency.

-Cataract,development deficiency and inental retardation because of Gulactital.

-Cirrhosis because of Galactose 1-phosphat gathering.

8.Pentoseoroticresones:

-xailouseReductuse low activity

نقش PPP در واکنش گلوتاتیون پراکسیداز اریتروسیتی

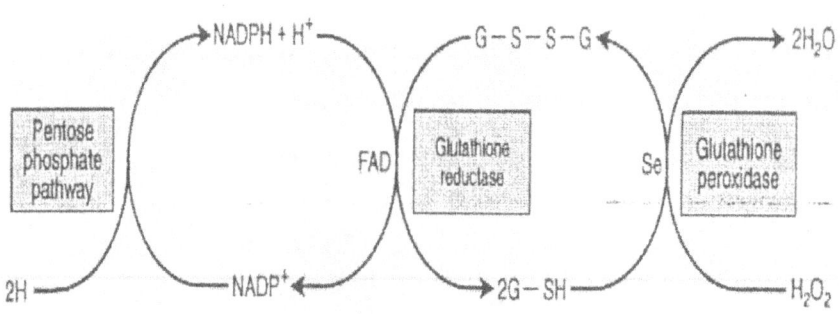

Figure 47: ppp role In GlutationproxicidaseErythroid reaction.

If xylose Reductase has increases so pentose phosphate pathway increases;Because the product which increases is pentose phosphate pathway primary matter.

TRANSFRRRIN(TRF)

Clinical importance

_Differential diagnosis of anemia(hypochorom microcytic anemia)

-Increase of TIBC and decrease of anemia(decrease of saturating percentage);Iron insufficiency anemia

-Decrease of TIBC and iron increasing (increase of saturating percentage);with iron-independent anemia(probably thalassemia)

Estrogen causes to increasing of TRF

$T_f$ (mg/dl) = 0.70 × TIBC (mg/dl)   TIBC=1043 × $T_f$

|  | G/L | Mg/dl |
|---|---|---|
| NEWBORN | 1.17-2.50 | 117-250 |
| ADULTS(20-60YR) | 2.0-3.6 | 200-360 |
| >60YR | 1.6-3.4 | 160-340 |

_In laboratory, transferrin considers with TIBC test

_Total iron binding capacity=TIBC

_Transferrin linkes to 2 Fe.

_In common state percentage of saturating is 33%.

$\left[\begin{array}{l}33\% \text{ two site} \\ 33\% \text{ one site} \\ 33\% \text{ no site}\end{array}\right.$ saturated.

**_The second name of TRF Is cedrofilin.**

_ It locates in B1 band, linkages to bivalent metals,

Synthesizes in liver and its synthesis is related to iron.

_It connects to 2 iron which is trivalent.

_Absorbed iron remains in intestine cell for 1-2 days ,then if throught these two days,body had needed to iron so iron absorptes but if did'nt need ,iron evacuates by feces.

_Iron that transportes by transferrin:

75% inters to Hb

10-20% inters to ferritin

5-15% inters to others reactions like as enzyme and cytochoromes.

_FeIII which connected to transferrin,also connects to Tra-receptors in surface of membrane.

_Tra receptors locates in state thatکوت شده with clotrine protein.

_After connecting of receptor-tra-Fe complex,endocytosis happens and he rate of PH in resulting endosome decreases to5-5.5 by means of $H^+$-ATPase pump.

_After decreasing of PH ,ironseprates from transferrin,trivalent iron is noxious for cell,so reductases to bivalent form by means ofacetipIII.

-Bivalent iron exites into cytoplasm by means of one transporter which names DMTI ,then receptor-transferrin complex returns to surface of cell again.

_Transferrin releases and receptor remains in surface of the cell.

_As endosome inters,DMTI also inters because there isclotrine in position.

**Vitamins:**

Vitaminsarea group oforganic nutrientsasmicrogramsormilligrams forhealth,growth and reproductionare required.

❖ these compounds inhumantissuescan not be made(exceptVitD)and mustreachthe bodybyfood.

❖ Vitk, Nicotinic acid, vit B2, vit B12, folic Acid B9aresynthesizedbyintestinal flora.

Vitamins and their derivatives often act as enzyme co-factors. vitaminco-factors requiredin terms ofcoenzymecalled.(cofactorsthataretightlyconnectedwith enzymes, prostheticgroupsare called.)

▪ intestinal bacteriawhichproducevitamins?

Theprostheticgroupcovalentlyattachedto theenzyme.

NAD as hydrogen and electron transfer and does not bind to the enzyme so that the transmitter.

FMN and FAD are the prosthetic group and covalently linked to the enzyme.

**deficiency of Vitamins:**

- The main causes of vitamin deficiency
  ○ insufficient removal Through the food
  ○ increase of excretion through of bleeding and diarrhea.

o insufficient absorption may be the result of obstruction of the bile ducts, diseases and intestinal disorders, Pernicious anemia (due to lack of intrinsic factor) is created.

o Insufficient use may result in the loss of a transporter proteins a specific vitamin in the serum and or defect convert a vitamin to the active form.

o Drugs that may induce a deficiency in vitamins including of that treatment with antibiotics or Alklsym that requires vitamins increases and drugs that interfere with food.

- Water-soluble vitamins

B groupe vitamins

B1(thiamine)

B2(riboflavin)

B3,niacin(nicotinic acid or nicotin amid)

B5(pantothenic acid)

B6(Piridoksin, piridoksamine, piridoksal)

B9(folic acide)

B12(kobalamin)

H(biotin)

C(Ascorbic acide)

**Thiamine (vitamin B1):**

has a key role in carbohydrate metabolism

-there are to form of thiamine triphosphate in peripheral nerve membrane.

-TPP is a coenzyme for several enzyme complexes that are responsible

for catalyze the oxidative decarboxylation reactions.

-in The pyruvate dehydrogenase complex is involved in the metabolism of carbohydrates.

-inThealfhaketoglutaratedehydrogenasecomplexis involvedinthe citric acid cycle.

- In the dehydrogenation of Ketoacid branched in the metabolism of leucine, isoleucine and valine is involved.

- in the transketolase in the pathwaye of pantose is involved.

- pyruvate dehydrogenase enzyemes and alpha ketoglutarate dehydrogenase consisting of 3 enzymes and there is 5coenzymeforactivity.( lipoate -COA- NAD , FAD , TPP) .

-Electrical stimulation of the nerves leading to loss of membrane TPP and Thiamine is released.

- possibly TPP In the nerves as a phosphate donorFor phosphorylation of the sodium channel transmitter In the nerve membrane acts.

**Thiamine deficiency leads to:**

❖ beriberi neuritis peripheral nerves that may be associated with cardiac damage and edema.

❖ fatal acute beriberi (shoshinberiberi) in which there is heart damage and metabolic disorders Without peripheral neuritis.

❖ wernicke's encephalopathy with korsakoff'spsychos that the effect of drugand alcoholabusewill happen.

❖ Oftalmoplegia: By shedding light into the eye pupil with no reaction.

❖ ataxia: wobble (like taking alcohol), have difficulty In the speaking.

❖ encephalopathy(alcoholinterfereswith theabsorption of vitaminB1).

❖

❖ anti-seizure drugs, such as barbiturates (anti-seizure) is applicable In the this case.

❖ neuritis: inflammation neuronal

❖ thiamine deficiency affects on the peripheral nervous system and the heart.

❖ thiamine deficiencysymptoms: mentaldisturbance, ataxia, and Oftalmoplegia.

**How can Discerned if a person is vitamin deficiency B1 or not?**

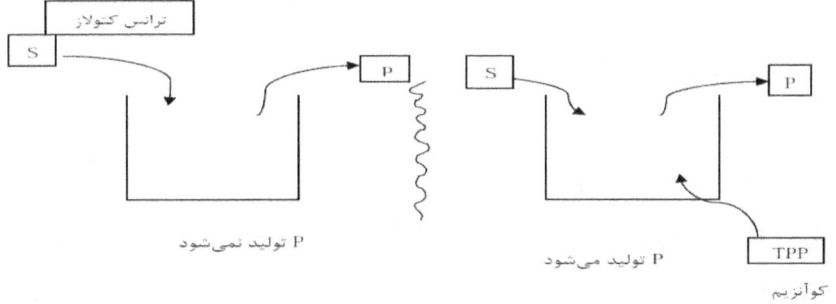

- Sowe have alack of vitamin B1butAgain adding vitamin do not have products and deficiency is caused by enzymes.

- The functional of vitamin B1 =Thiazodium.

-An importantpartof the vitamin B1, theC-ring thatactsas areactant.

**Nutritional statusof thiamine:**

❖ activation apotransketolaseresulting from erythrocyte destruction by addition of thiamine diphosphate in reaction to the environment Invitro as a Index Nutritional status of thiamine is used.

**Riboflavin(vitaminB2):**

Riboflavin its role In the metabolism plays as a coenzymethat that includes:

Flavin mononucleotide (FMN) Flavin adenine dinucleotide (FAD)

Isoalloxazine rings is composed of dimethylbenzene and petrine , to the NLoa Ribitol is connected.

Yellow color B-complex is due to B2.

Vitamin B2 includes the portions of: 1-dimethylbenzene  2- petrine   3- Ribito

--------------???????/Bonds of one of two dubleabsorb light and color to yellow.

Coenzyme Adehydrogenaseare.

Milk and dairy products are the main dietary sources of riboflavin.

In acid solutions, are stable but unstable alkali.

Coenzyme flavin as electron carriers oxidation in the reduction reactions in mitochondrial respiratory chain is involved. Flavin oxidase play an important role in the body overall oxidative stress.

**Riboflavin shortage:**

riboflavinis involvedinirontransport.

RiboflavinintoFADandFMNtoreduce.

hypothyroidism Riboflavin into FAD and FMN to reduce.

The main symptoms of riboflavin deficiency isShylose, falsi dermatitis and glossitis.

riboflavinnutritional statusby measurementof erythrocyteglutathione reductase activity(with the addition of FADinIn Vitro)is carried out.

نحوه عمل FAD در انتقال الکترون

Mode of Action FAD in electron transfer

VitaminB3 (Niacin):

o  Because thisvitamin in the bodyis madeofTryptophan, It can not befullyconsideredas a vitamin.

o  conversion oftryptophan toniacinin the bodyis low.

o  for the Synthesis of niacin requires vitamins B2, B6, and iron.

o  nicotinic acid and nicotin amide are Biologically active form of niacin in the body.

o  Its biological activity to form Nicotinamide ring there is In the co-enzymes NAD and NADP, and involved in redox reactions. In the tryptophan pathway, B3 produced.

o  Always the body does not produce tryptophan from the B3.to produce B3, much material are needed Which is not affordable.

o  Pellagra(Photosensitive dermatitis)is causedby adeficiency oftryptophanand niacin.

o  Itsdeficiencyis causingdermatitis, diarrhea, dementia andglossitis.

o  Pellagra can be caused is the result of Hartnup disease, Despite a Suitable harvest food-tryptophan and niacin also occur.

o  Nicotinicacidis usedto treathyperlipidemia, which causesdilation ofbloodvesselsandopenthem.

o  Taking more than 500mg / dl nicotine and nicotinic acid amide can cause liver damage.

•  Hartnup : Disease in which the absorption of amino acids monoamine and monoacidic in the intestine and Reabsorption in the kidney is impaired(The most important amino acid that can be disrupted, is tryptophan) . B3, the vessel expands and effects on lipid (plaques) lacking.

**Which of the vitamins are water soluble toxicity**? Niacin

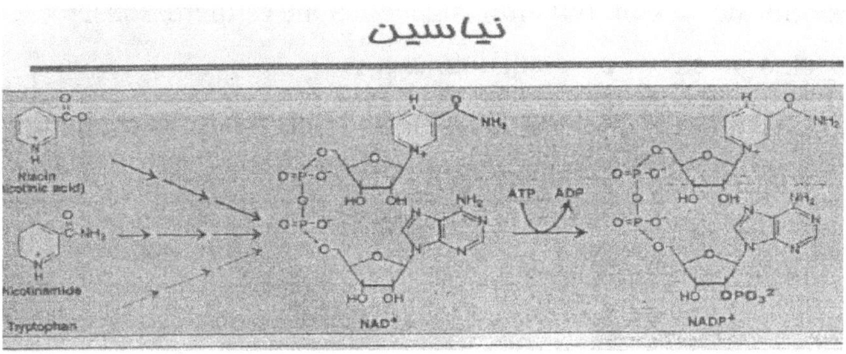

نیاسین

- Isnicotinecigarettes asvitamins? Isthe increaseinbodyB3is addictive?

**Biotine:**

o Coenzyme R or Vitamin H there is in these cases : urea, Valeric acid and tetrahydrothiophene

o This vitamin has been formed form tetrahydrothiophene ring andaureagroup.

o Thiophene ring has Valeric acid as a side chain.

o as a coenzyme Carboxylase enzyme acts .

o Widely distributed in foods.

o By normal bowel flora is synthesized.

o Avidin (an antivitamins) found in egg whites and if eat much of it, can cause biotin deficiency.

o Avidin in the digestive tract binds to biotin and prevents its absorption .

o    Falcidermatite, hair loss, anorexia, depression andhyperchloremia,in the effect of lack of vitamin H, arise.One reasonforthe lack ofHvitamin,is genetic.One of thereasonsis thelack ofan enzyme calledBiotinase.

o    Vitamin H attached to lysine and Schiff base is created.

o    Acetyl-CoA carboxylase (in the fat synthesis) has the highest rate of H.

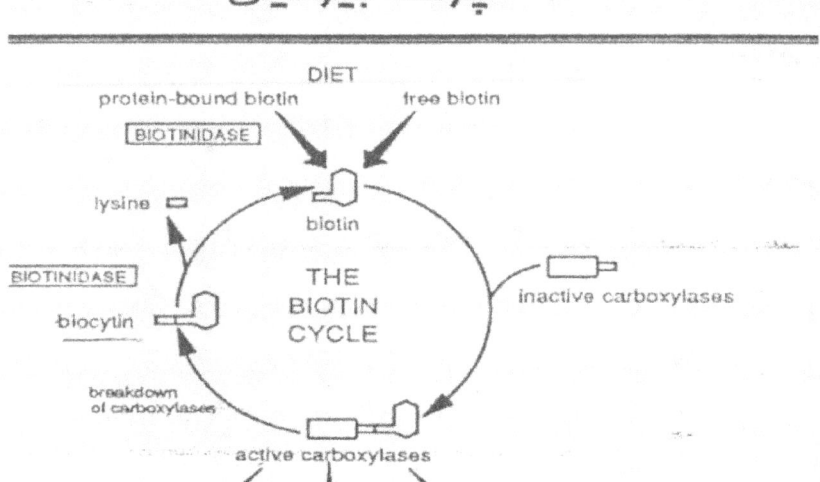

چرخه بیوتین

Biotin is enter to the body and in to enzymes that need it.Whenconnectedandworkdone, separated.

If to the lysine roots of biotin , lysine connected, This combinationwillsaybiosytin, which biotinidase enzyme, separated the lysine and activated vitamin H .

**pantothenic acid:**

o   Consisting of D-peptide of beta-alanine and butyric acid.

o   Is the part a ofCoenzymeA andacylcarrier groups(ACP).

o   In the liver, the binding of ATP and cysteine, co-enzyme A is made.

--CoAin thesynthesis andoxidation of fatty acids, acetylationandsynthesischolostrolinvolved.

--ACPparticipatesinthe synthesis offatty acids.

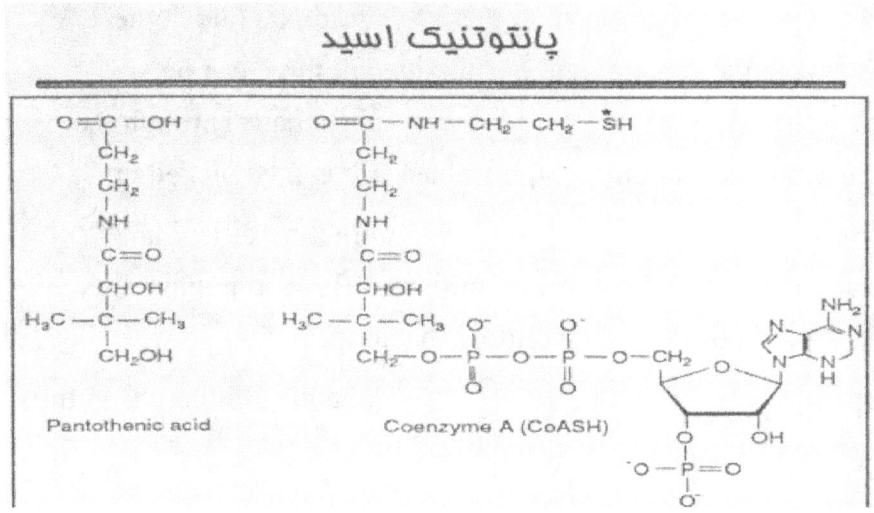

## ساختار ویتامین B6

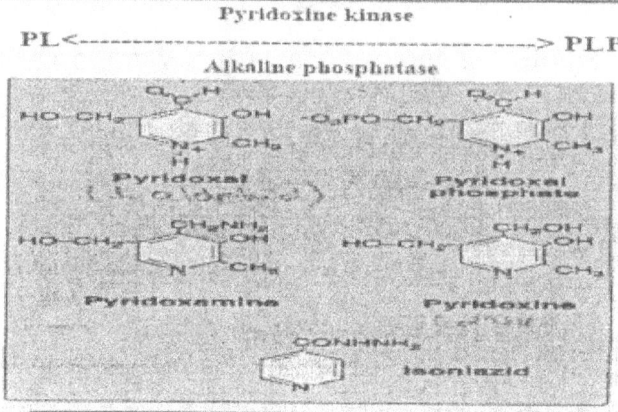

❖ pyridoxal (aldehydes), Pyridoxamin (amine) and pyridoxine, all three can be phosphated. phosphate Through the kinase binds and through phosphatase It can be picked up.

❖ structure of Isoniazid (tuberculosis medication) is similar to B6 And impairs the production of B6 in tuberculosis bacteria.

❖ Vitamin B6 there is in the transaminase And glycogenphosphorylase B6.

o Pyridoxal, pyridoxine, pyridoxamine and their phosphate derivatives 5, there are B6 activity.

o 80% of total body vitamin B6 to form pyridoxal phosphate In muscles With glycogen phosphorylase enzyme exists.

❖ pyridoxalphosphateisacoenzyme.

❖ vitamin B6, in metabolism of amino acids, Particularly involved in transamination and decarboxylation.

❖ Pyridoxalphosphate,is cofactor of glycogen phosphorylase .

❖ Reduced glucose tolerance as a result of Vitamin B6 deficiency is caused.

❖ Vitamin B6is involvedin thesynthesisneurotransmitters.

❖ Vitamin B6inthe structure ofserotonin, epinephrine, norepinephrine, and GABAis involved.

❖ Vitamin B6also plays a roleinconvertinghomocysteinetocysteine.

❖ Vitamin B6 deficiency, results in increased homocysteine (hyperhomocysteinemia) and increase the risk of cardiovascular disease.

❖ Homocysteine is a toxic and dangerous; B6 deficiency causes heart disease.

❖ Vitamin B6 in steroid hormone activity, picked up binding Hormone-receptor complex in the DNA TO activity of this hormone in the end.

❖ The deficiency of Vitamin B6, ensitivity to estrogens, androgens, cortisol and vitamin D increases.

- Some medicines may interfere with the absorption of vitamin B6, which include:

-Penicillamine (used to treat rheumatoid arthritis and cystinuria)

-Isoniazid (Treatment of Tuberculosis)

**Assessment of nutritional status of vitamin B6:**

-With the addition of pyridoxal phosphate to the medium containing erythrocyte aminotransferases done.

• Vitamin B6 can cause picked of steroid hormone of the genes.

❖ B6 is a coenzyme in the metabolic pathway kynureninase. persons, consum the treptophan and urine check out. If tryptophan was repelledThispathwayis impaired.Andvitamin B6there is no.Orhasrun its course and producesketoadipatex.

❖ Iftryptophanincreases, Theeffect ofvitamin B6deficiency, Kynorenynazpathwaywill be not made.And3-hydroxi kinorin (One pathway metabolites Trptophan)isconverted intoxezantoronatand Excretedin the urine.

3-Hydroxykynurenine

↓ NH₄⁺

Xanthurenate

## Kobalamin B-12:

❖ In saliva to the Kobalofilin connected.

❖ to the Intrinsic factor (Intrinsic factor, Apoarytryn) in the stomach, binds. Intrinsic factor is a glycoprotein small that Bycells inthe mucosaliningthe stomach(parietal cells) secreted. Uptake through receptors in the terminal ileum (lower part of the intestine) that bound to the complex of vitamin B12 and intrinsic factor to be done.

## The two main function ofcobalamin:

1-stimulated growth   2-stimulated maturation ofred blood cells

❖ Cobalamin is like a circle of Heme That instead of iron, there is cobalt .

❖ In vitamin B-12, Fourcapacity to the N and fivecapacity to the dimethylBnzonydazol and six capacity to the CN, CH3, 5-deoxiyadnozine and cobalamine may be connected and

Alternativenameswill be found.the sixthcapacitydeterminesWhich partgoes.

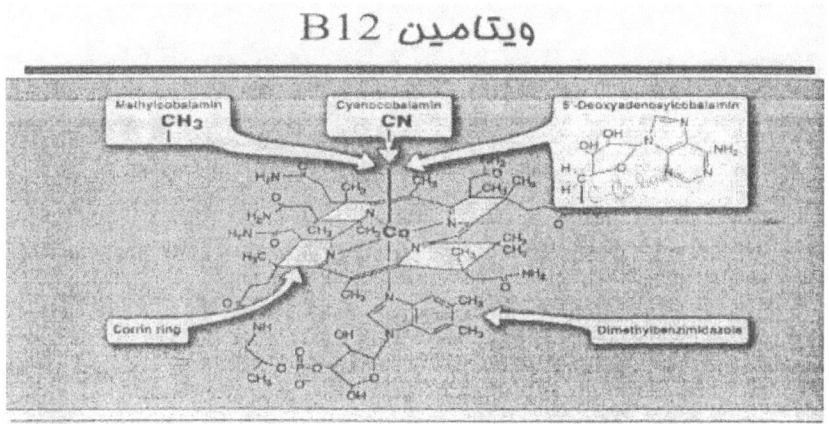

ويتامين B12

**Transport ofvitamin B12:**

- Cobalamin in blood Connected to the trans-cobalamin II Transported to the liver and other tissues.
- In the liver with connect to thetrans-cobalaminstored.
- Ashydroxycobalaminentersthecell.
- in the cytosol converted to the Methylcobalamin.
- Inthe mitochondriato form5-doxycyclineadenosylcobalaminenters.

## جذب ویتامین B12

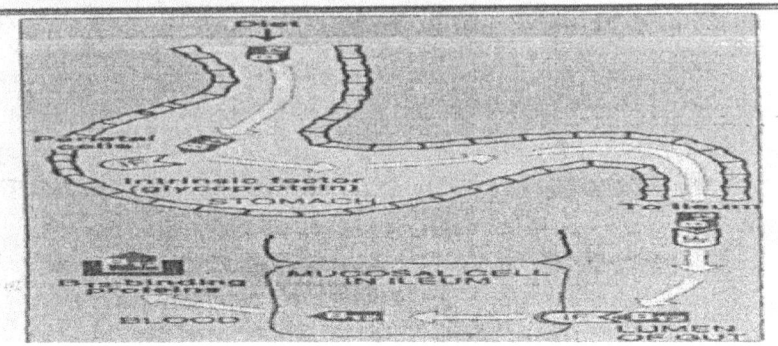

## واکنش هایی که کوبالامین در آنها نقش دارد

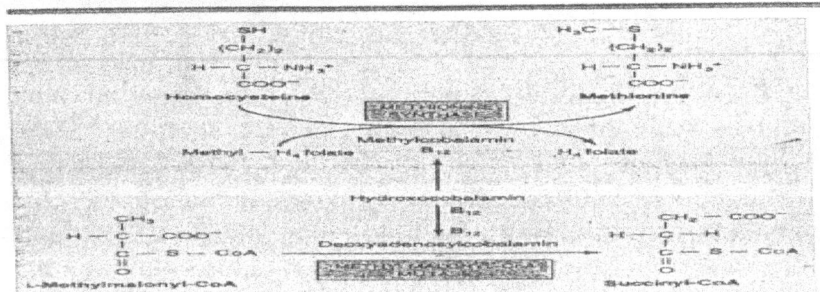

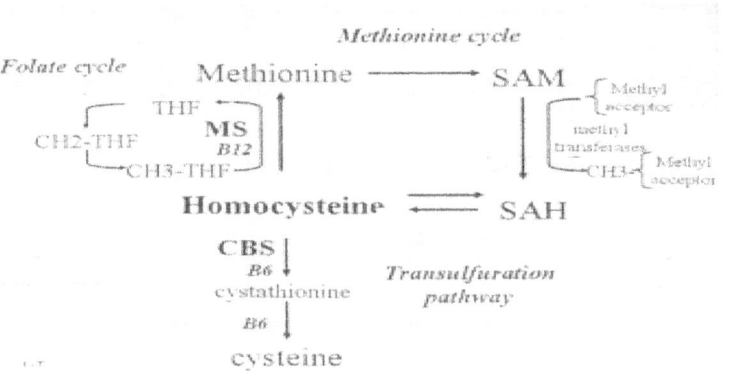

## Cobalamin deficiency:

The most commoncauses ofdeficiencyincludethe following:

1- badabsorbing

2-atrophic gastricmucosa.

3-terminal ileum disease.

### cobalamin deficiencyreasons:

1- anemiaPersynoz

2- Demyelinationof nerve fibersgrewSpinal cord(Especially the dorsaland lateralcolumns)

## Vitamin B9:

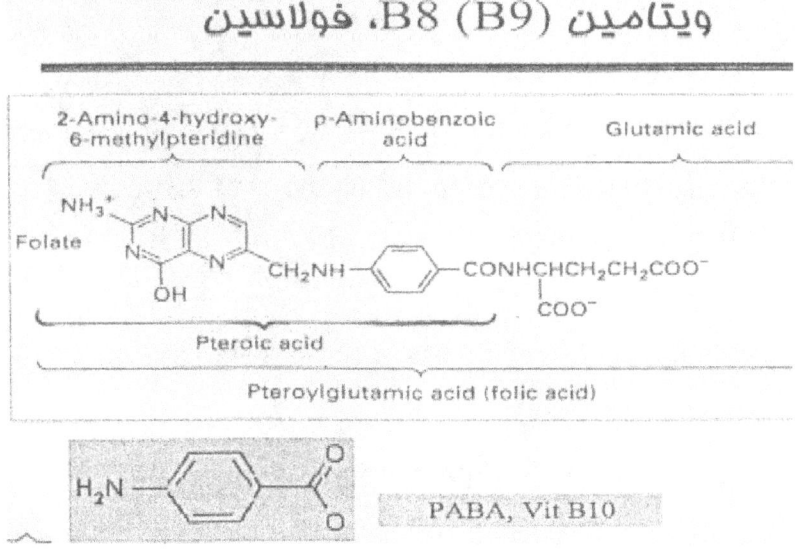

ويتامين (B9) B8، فولاسين

| Pteroyl Glvami c acid | Pterioc acid | فولات (پتریدین) PABA (قبلاً BLO می‌گفتند) اسید ** گلوتامیک |

The active form of folic acid (glutamic acid Ptroyyl) is the tetrahydrofolate (THF).

- active form of vitamin B9 in the body is THF.

- Vitamin B9 is involved in the synthesis of thymidine Since CH3 adds, then metabolism of DNA (but not RNA) disrupted.

- Vitamin B9 in the synthesis of purines and Pyrimidin and in formation of DNA is required.

- Vitamin B9 is involved in erythrocyte maturation.

- antiepileptic drugs and Contraceptive drugs are reduced folate.

**Dysfunctionalfolate:**

- in The effect of vitamin B12 deficiency occurs.
- retained of folate to form methyl tetrahydrofolate.
- folate Functional deficiency because vitamin B12 deficiency, becauce in the case of B12 deficiency methyl-THF is failed,so to active form of H4 folat not become active, Therefore not able to switch to other forms, We have only methyl tetrahydrofuran, So we have a dysfunctional folate.

**Folate deficiencycauses:**

Megaloblasticanemia and leukemia

- Folic acid deficiency (or cobalamin) affects on cell proliferation of high-speed .These cellsare requiredto providethymidinein DNA synthesisof these twovitaminsareneeded. These factors with effects on the bone marrow may cause megaloblasticanemia .
- Folicacid deficiencymakescellsgrowandmegaloblastic anemiaoccurs.Forsynthesis, DNA, B9 and B12are needed.So when these factors do not exist, DNA are not synthesized, As a result of,largecells,Butthere is noDNAthat Divisionoccur.

## نقص عملکردی فولات

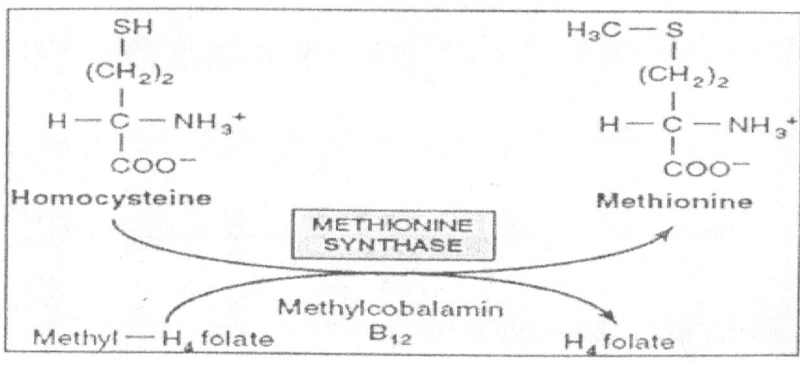

## فولات

The different folate coenzymes are specific for particular reactions.

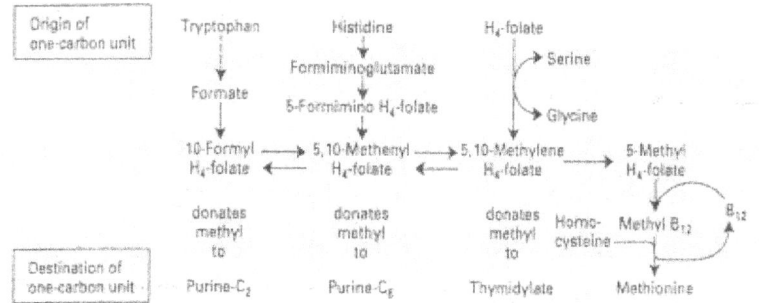

## آنمی مگالوبلاستیک

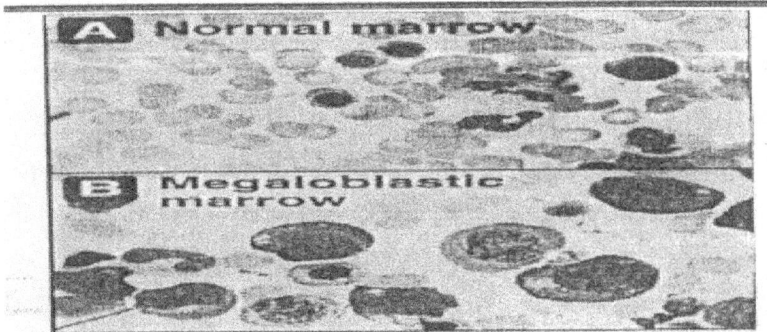

درمان بیماری با استفاده از مهار سنتز فولات

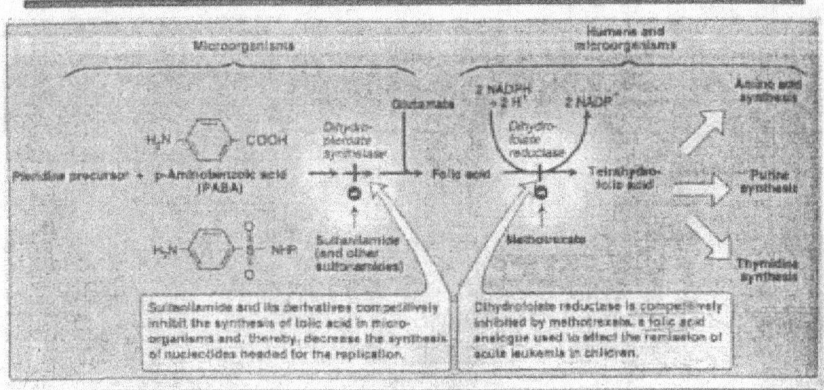

**Nutritionalanemiacategories:**

1- Microcyticanemia

2- normositer (the body does not consume enough calories and protein )(nutritional deficiencies).

In this case thecells are normal, but RBCis low. Lowhemoglobinandhaveanemia.

3- macrocytic(cell is large)

- Bacteria are produced , folic acid, B6 and B12.

- Our bodies does not the enzyme that antibiotic inhibits, Folicacidand B6are suppliedfrom the outside, so antibioticshave noeffecton humans.

methotrexate drug cause inhibition tetra hydro folate reductase enzyme. Which thisdrugsusedinchemotherapy.

**Folate deficiencycauses:**

- Neural Tube Defects

Fetalneuraltube defectsare associatedwithlow folate levels.

- Hyperhomocysteinemia

o Homocysteine increases the risk of cardiovascular disease, atherosclerosis, hypertension thrombus is associated.

o Homocystinuriato the sources offolate, cobalaminandpyridoxinesometimesreactingthe show.

**Ascorbate:**

- Is aregenerativeagent.
- In Thereaction of Regenerativeoxidationandelectron transferis involved.
- Involvedin the synthesis ofkondroitinsulfat.
- Plays a rolein the formation ofcollagenhydroxyproline.
- In wound healing, biosynthesis neurotransmitters (dopamine) and in immune function plays a role.
- Ther are Inlocusit, adrenal, pituitary and brainconcentrationsplentiful.
- Long-term preservationand cookingislikely to causethe loss ofvitamins.

**Necessity ofascorbateinvarious tissues:**

- Gums, arteriesand othersoft tissuesand bones (colagen synthesis)
- PerformanceNerves (Noronransmyterand hormones)
- NutrientMetabolism (Especiallyiron, protein and fat)
- actinganti-oxidant andfree radicalCollection (Directlyand byactivating thevitamin E)

**Ascorbatedeficiency:**

**Vitamin C deficiencycancauseScurvy; Scurvysymptoms:**

- Bleedinggums andteeth.
- swollen and painfuljoints.
- Poorwoundhealing
- dizziness andfatigue.
- The loss ofsafetyfunction
- We have justseeninalcoholicsandthe elderly.
- upset stomach,intestineand kidney stones
- Excessive consumption ofascorbate(taking more than 200mgper day) could beScurvy.

- Vitamin C by cooking, preservation disappears.
- Vitamin C can cause interference with copper metabolism.
- Vitamin C if taken more than needed, and toxicity.
- In people who have kidney stones, vitamin C should not be used.
- Oxalate stones are one of the reasons for their creation, vitamin-C.

**Fat-soluble vitamins:**

- Vitamin A (retinol)
- Vitamin D (cholecalciferol)
- Vitamin E (tocopherol)
- Vitamin K (Phytonadione)

**Vitamin A:**

Vitamin A activity of two classes of compound are obtained as follows:

- retinol and its derivatives (retinoic acid retinaldehyde)
- carotenoid compounds

**beta-Carotene:**

- Beta-carotene is a Pro-Vitamins, that are Converted to retinol And to form retinol palmitate Stored in the liver and there are in plants.
- Each molecule of beta-carotene Two retinol molecules are created.

- Each moleculeof alpha-carotene Only onemolecule ofretinolare created.

- Food sources include liver, butter, vegetables and milk fortified.

**RoleinSight:**

- Retinolin the retinaConvertedtorhodopsin.

-Retinal with A protein called Opsin, in thecylindricalcellsis formed of rhodopsin and inCones cells formed of yodopsina.

-Preferably,thecisisomerarelinkedoptsin.

- Light absorption, stimulate and reshapetheopsin and converted the Isomers cis-retinal to form all-trans andThatis weaklyconnectedto theopsin.

- The result of thischangeretinaldehyderclcascof theopsinAndan action potentialisgenerated.

- Al-trans-retinal is a messagenervous.

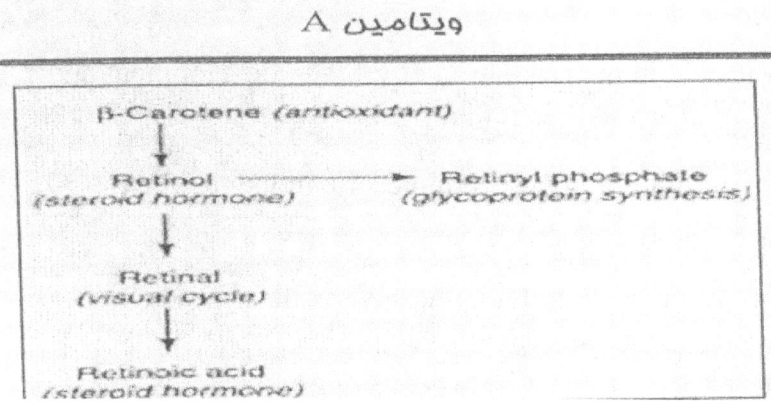

## ویتامین A

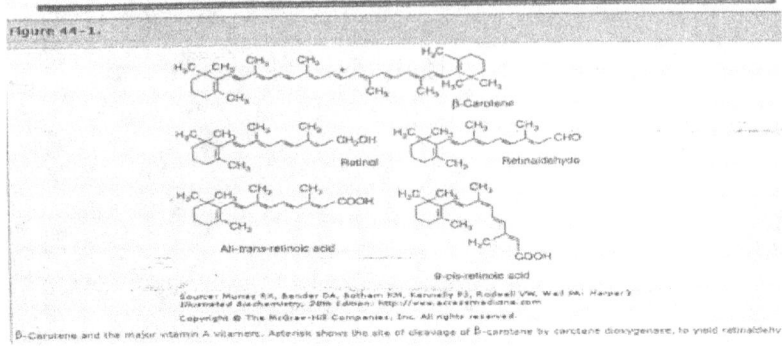

## نقش در بینایی

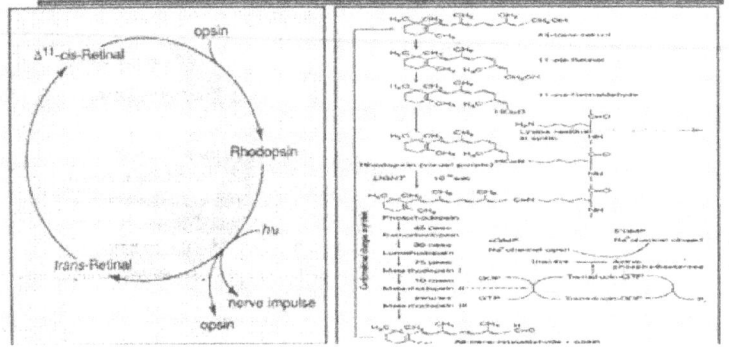

**Retinoic acid:**

-Retinoic acid in the regulation of growth, development and differentiation of tissues involved.

-Such assteroid hormones, retinoicacidbinding to nuclearreceptor(RxR, RAR).

-Vitamin Aappearstoepithelialtissue growth, reproduction andbone growthis needed.

- Retinol and retinoic acid are involved in the synthesis of creatine and transferrin.

transferrin deficiency ⟶ anemia

Creatine deficiency ⟶ Probably plays a role in infection.

**Vitamin A deficiency can cause the following:**

**Defect in vision**

Progressive The type of night blindness and complete blindness.

The loss of tissue in the eye and eyestrain (Exoftalmia)

**Skin lesions:**

Follicular hyperkeratosis caused by vitamin A deficiency, which causes a horn and scaling of the skin.

**Sexual dysfunctions:**

- Gonadal dysfunction in men
- Abortion in Women

**Anemia:**

-Due to defects in the synthesis of transferrin.

**Increased susceptibility to infection:**

Due to excessive keratin synthesis.

**Vitamin A toxicity:**

-Toxicity in the Eatingtoo muchvitamin Aoccurs, especially inchildren.

-Liverand spleenWithlargelipid-filled macrophages(Hepatomegaly and Splenomegaly).

- Long-term toxicity can cause cirrhosis.
Earlysymptomsinclude: headache,excitement,extremeflexibilityand bone pain.

- High doses of synthetic derivatives of retinoic acid, is teratogenic (causing genetic changes in the fetus).

-Additional carotene is benign and causes discoloration and Jaundice-like skin.

- Most toxicvitamin,is a vitamin.

**Vitamin A:**

-Vitamin Dis neededonlywhenapersonisdeprivedofsunlight.

- Vitamin Dis synthesizedinthe skinbyultravioletlight.

- 7-Dehydrocholesterol be converted to Cholecalciferol.

- Cholecalciferol is a precursor 1,25-dihydroxycholecalciferol, Plays a roleinregulatingthe absorptionofcalcium homeostasis.

**The main functionof vitamin D:**

-$Ca^{2+}$ and phosphatehomeostasis

- Stimulate intestinal absorption of calcium (by stimulating the synthesis calbindin).

- calcification and prepare the bone.

- Decrease␣renal excretion of calcium.

- Vitamin D hormone is : calcitriol (Occurs in the liver and kidney)

- Too much vitamin D is toxic. More calcium is absorbed and In the tissues caused by Ksytvz and Kidney stones are caused.

- In Children Rickets caused by vitamin D deficiency That is associated with the deformation of long bones.

- In adults Its deficiency causes osteomalacia or rickets.

- Corticosteroids, disabled the vitamin D.

- Vitamin D is toxic in excess amounts And the increase in plasma calcium, resulting in soft tissue calcification It also provides the groundwork for the formation of kidney stones.

## ويتامين D

## ويتامين D

- 25-hydroxylation in liver and 1-hydroxylation in kidney occurs.

- Vitamin D Resistant Rickets is: do not be a hydroxylation in the liver and kidneysAnd does not produce hormones. Rickets in liver and kidney disorders at the progress being made.

**Vitamin-E:**

- the Major sources include vegetables and oilseeds (sunflower, corn, and soybeans).

- Vitamin E is not metabolized in the body.

- Vitamin E is the most important natural antioxidants.

- the First line of defense against peroxidation of unsaturated fatty acids in phospholipids of cell membranes and within the cell.

- Vitamin E is a generic name for the family are called tocopherols and Tocotrienol (Vitamer, other forms of Vitamin say).

- Alpha-Tocopherol is the most active of these compounds.

- Tocopherol is usually concentrated in a cluster of lipid structures that are expose to high-pressure of $O_2$.

- Vitamin E there are in the membranes of red blood cells and membranes of the respiratory tract and the retina.

- Vitamin E prevents the oxidation of LDL.

- While increasing intake of polyunsaturated fatty acids, The need for vitamin E increases.

- Vitamin E is a fat-soluble antioxidant And there is in the plasma membrane and plasma lipoproteins.

- Vitamin E in the Fat-soluble vitamins Has the lowest toxicity.

**Free radicals and antioxidants:**

Free radicals are compounds with unpaired electrons that are highly active and have a tendency to oxidize other substances.

- Antioxidantchemical compound that Easilyoxidizedand preventstheoxidation ofother compounds.

**Tocopherol:**

the type of alpha Against Particles of oxygen active And gamma are resistant to the active ingredient of nitrogen.

The type of GammaInthe prevention ofatherosclerosisIs more effectivethanalpha.

**Vitamin E deficiency:**

It iscausederythrocytehemolysis. (These cells havethe ability toprotect againstoxidation).

-Causeweakness, loss of muscle and creatinine urea.

- Increasedbreakdownof musclecells.

- Causesof infertilityAndanemia.

- Pregnant and lactating womenandinfants in the diet needs to moretocopherol that Possibledeficiencyof vitaminA do notcauseanemia.

**Vitamin K:**

Three classes ofcompoundsContains of vitamin Kactivity:

K1 or filokuinon(Fresh vegetables, especially broccoliand spinach)

K2 or menakuinon(Intestinal bacteria, butter, liver and eggs).

**The most activeform ofvitamin K:**

K3orMenadiol(synthetic), dissolved in water.

**Function:**

Activation of importance proteins in thecoagulation.

Prothrombin(factorII-) proconvertin(factor-VII) christmas factor(factor-IX) stuart power factor(factor-X).

**warfarindicoumarol:**

Anticoagulanttherapy forpatients withhigh risk ofcoronaryarterythrombosis, coagulationactivation.

gamma carboxylation be caused. in the all of them there are Glutamic acid and that to the end of all Their COO adds.

**VitaminK deficiency:**

Newborn infantsmay bedeficientinit.PairPoorabilitytotransportlipids.

Phylloquinone

Menaquinone

Menadiol

Menadiol diacetate (acetomenaphthone)

Source: Murray RK, Bender DA, Botham KM, Kennelly PJ, Rodwell VW, Weil PA: Harper's Illustrated Biochemistry, 28th Edition: http://www.accessmedicine.com

**Vitamin K**

There below compounds have vitamin k activity :

$K_1$ or philocinoun (fresh vegetables specially cabbage and spinach)

$K_2$ or menacinoun (intestine bacteria,butter,liver and egg)

The most active form of vitamin k

$K_3$ or menadeole (artificial) is solotion in water .

Revenue :

Activation of important proteins in coagulation

-protambin (factor II),procanourtin (factore V II)

Christmas factore (Ix factore),Bavor-stevarthfactore (x factor)

Varfarin (Dicomaroulc)

-Anti conclusion drugs uses for cure of persons which have high risk of heart vessels trumbosis.

Activation of conclusion factor.causestheir.

8-Crboxylation.all of them have glutamic acid which connected to their end coo⁻

Vitamin k deficit :

Probably has seens in newborn babies.

Placenta has low ability in Lipid transfer.

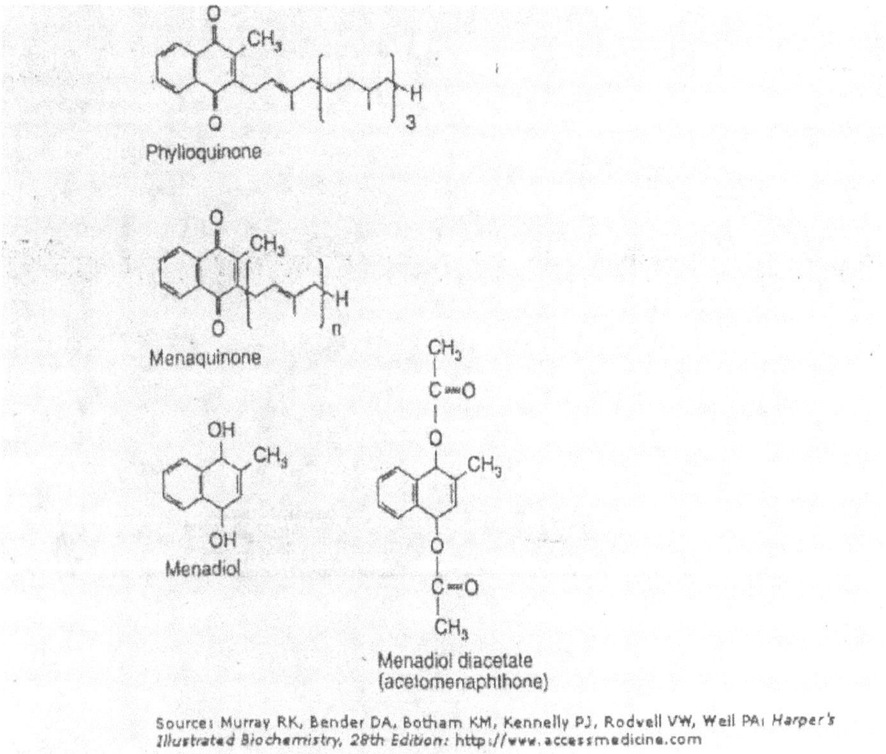

Figure 68 :phylloquinone,Menaquinone and Menadiol structure

Fatness in absorption syndrome :

Both platelets wall and II ,VII,IX,X factors have negative electricity.calcium connected to these two negative electricities and creates clot in bloodshed region.

## نقش ویتامین K در انعقاد

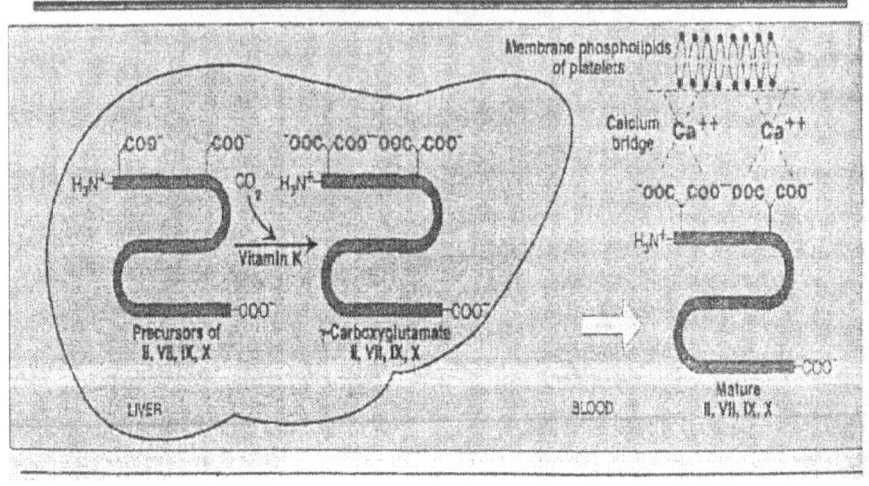

# نقش ویتامین K در انعقاد

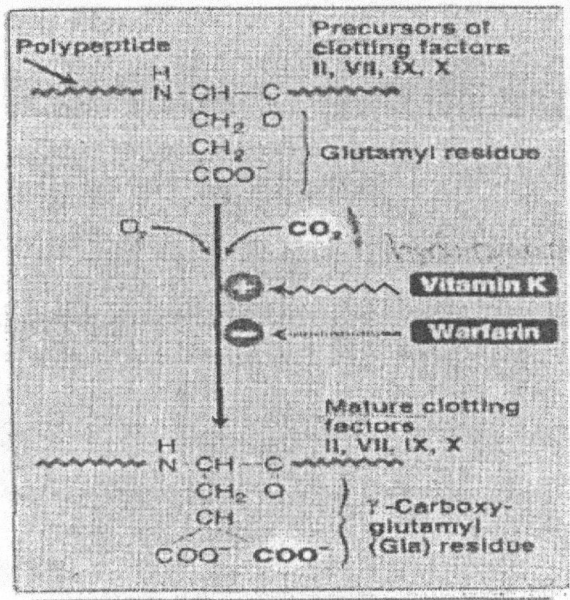

Figure 69: vitamin k role in coagulation

**Plasma proteins** :

Percentage amount of various WBC cells is different due to person situation, age desease which is as follows :

50-70%

2-4%

Less than 1%

20-30%

2-8%

## ترکیبات خون کامل

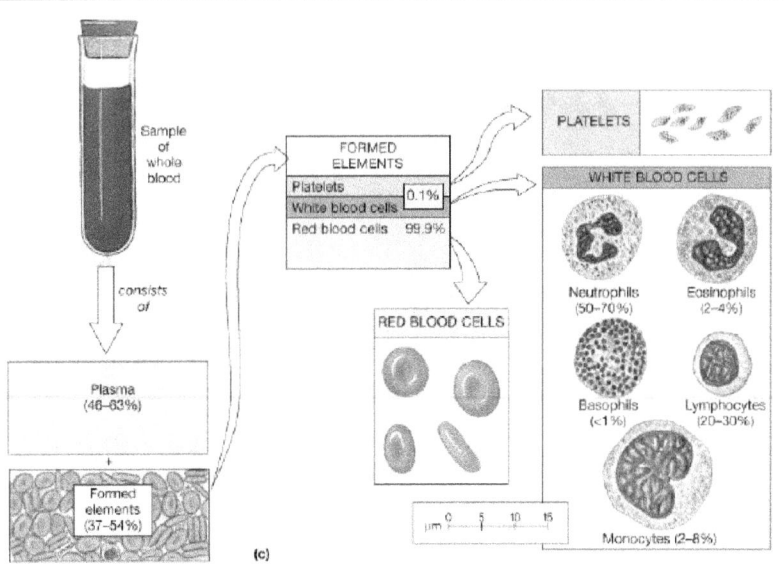

Figure 70 : Total blood compounds

1.Albumin (Al):

Primary synthesis of Albumin is eclipsed of COP(plasma colloidal osmotic pressure).

Albumin's main role is osmotic pressure regulating.

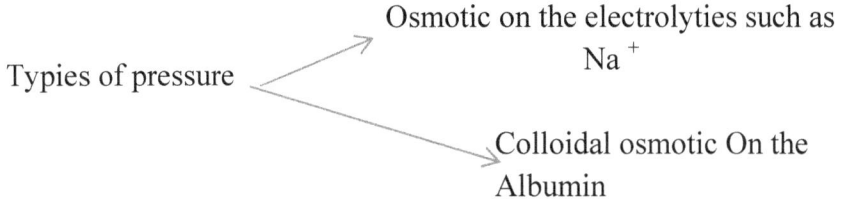

Secondary synthesis of Albumin is eclipsed of proteins amount

Albumin synthesis has decreased eclipsed of cytokinines and hypo callmia.

Albumin catabolize :

Albumin has both pinocytosis and catabolism in tissues. Amino acides which result from albumin uses for protein synthesis of thosetissues.few albumin enters to GI and peroximale cells reabsorbes a few percentage of albumin, breaks it,then have repeles it from urine.

Pinocytosis :vesicules which had created in material around the cell and entered to cell.

It is shown in bellowing figure :

## آلبومین

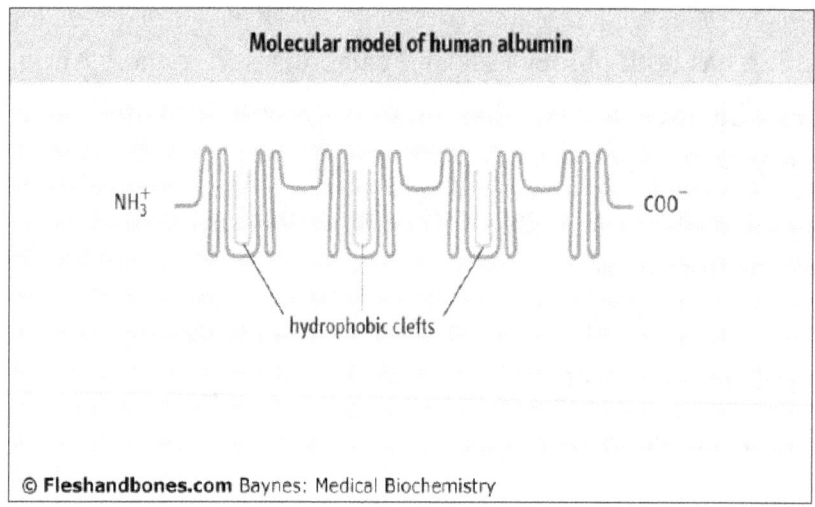

Figure 71: Albumin structure

## تنظیم فشار کولوئیدی

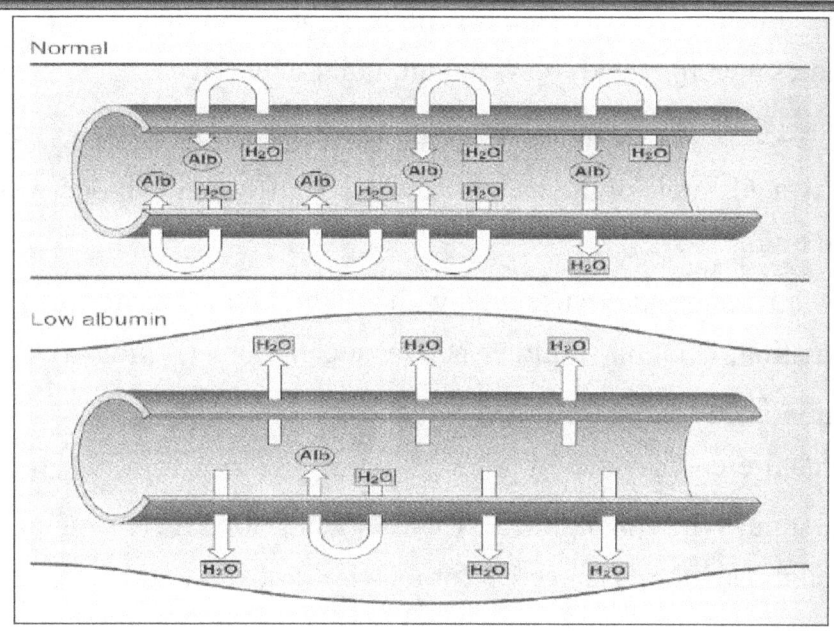

Figure72: colloidal pressure regulating

Pressure is high in artery.material especially water passes easily,enters to midolletissuesespace,middletissuse water increased then returnes to vessel again because of albumin presence.because albumin remains in blood and reabsorbs water in the vein.

Encothycpressure,sodium helps to water reabsorbing inner the vein.

Albumin has differential aminoacids(hydrophilic amphipatic,hydrophobic) so connected to various material and serves like as transferor in blood some of these material are as follows :

Hematine,Aspirine,bilirubin(connected bilirubin to albumin names unconjugated),polar and unipolar material.

When sugar has synthesised,albumin connected to it.

fatty acid is one of the materials which transferred to blood with albumin.

10-fatty acids had transefered with albumin.after transferring of glutation,Albumin would be active such as an antioxidant.

Aminoacid source for protein synthesizing is in the circumferential tissue.

Albumin synthesizing increased after using food.Increasing of albumin synthesis is needed for material transfer to the tissue.

Increased aminoacids of food,which enters to liver,used as albumin synthesis and both other aminoacids and side material had been transferred to tissues.

Clinical importance of albumin :

Increasing ⟶ Acute Dehydration

Decreasing ⟶ unalbuminamia

Decreasing of in flasmmation happens for four reseanswhich are as follos :

1.Homodylation

2.Intering to outer vesels space

3.Increased consumption

4. Decreased synthesis

-liver disease

-Increasing of repelling :urine ,Gl

-malnutrition

Reference Intervals Albumin : 3.5 to 5.2 g/dl because of Albumin increasing,total protein increased.(because 70% of blood is protein)

-unalbuminamia : Gene has deficiency,Albumin dose not synthesis, maybe changed albumin serves as main albumin so body activation because of albumin,s absence had diminished.

In inflammation,because of heighcytocynes production , synthesizing of albumin decreased in liver.

In inflammation:Blood cell takes their needed protein form outer part of vesselsalbumin which the vessels also takes their needed protein from inner vein Albumin.

Because of production Both histamine and circular amins,ininflammation,cells had contracted and inner tissuse space increased,so arrival of Albumin in this space increases.

Hepatic desease : Albumin is one of the most important factors in LFT test.

Homodylation: it happens because of blood diluting.

In nephritis syndrome:Albumin has decreased,because of peroximal cells deficiency.

In diabetes : Blood sugar increased,positive charges has covering the septum(there is cyalice acid in septum)of glumeroule,so repelling of albumin increases.

In Hematoria : Repelling albumin increasing happens.because of fever and intensive exercise,amount of albumin decreased.

2.Alpha1-acid Glycoprotein (orosmucoid)(AAG):

-Amount of both carbohydrate and acid cyalice is hiegh.

-AAG synthesis fulfilled agency of hepatic.

-In inflammation: In addition to liver, AAB synthesizing agency of ,monocytes.

-Catabolism: Hepatic receptors takes AAGs.

-AAGs demi-consonant:three days.

-AAG is an lipocalyne(are materials which connected to fatness and transfers them.)that connected to lipophilice material.

Other members of group which are Lipocaline are as follows :

RBP

$\alpha_1$microglobulin

βLactoglobulin

-It causes to connection and disabling of both alkalice and lipophilic compounds.such as progesterone and realated hormones.

It also,cause to connection to druges like as propranolol, ,cowinidin,coleriromazin,bansodioasines ,cocaine.

-AAGs are connected material to progesterone and other hormones which remain connected to them until needed time for the transposition and causes:

1. Decrease reaction of Immunesystem
2. phagocytosis decreasing agency of Nutrophilies.
3. Halter of plateletal gathering.
4. Halter of mitosis.
5. formation of fiberes.
6. Lipo protein Lipase cofactor

The most important accomplishment of AAG is that is uses like as cofactor.

APOC is another cofactor of LPL.

Clinical importance :     Increase:

_collitceratio

-Hormones;Increase eclipsed of glycocorticoiedes(with $HP^+$ and pre-albumin).

-Glycocoriticoled causes to,IncreaseAAG,$Hp^+$ and pre-albumin synthesis but sterogene decreases AAG synthesis.

Acute phase Response (ARR):

-In tissual necrosis and inflammation increases three-four fold.

-Ammount of AAG has increased (it means that AAG is positive-ARP)

Decrease :

-SterogeneHormon

-Sieving protein Loss like as Nefurathic syndrome Reported amount In statistical community:

Reference Intervalse : 0.5 to 1.2

Because AAG includes heigh carbohydrate and acidcyalice so it does not accept proteinaceouseoulors in electrophore sis so must uses carbohydratalcoulors like as PAS (periodic acid pass).

Molecular weight of AAG is 40 kD and carbohydrate amount is 45%.

3. Alpha 1-Antitrypsin(AAT):

-It synthesis in liver and includes three carbohydratal chain.

-It is an Acute phase protein.

Catabolism :

-Raising of AAT-enzyme ayency of special hepatic receptor.

-Raising of AAT.

-Demi-consonant:six-seven days.

-Amount of its carbohydrate is low and it is the most basic protein of $α_1$-group.

Catabolism happens in two ways:

1. when connected to enzyme,enzyme complex and $α_1$ transfers to liver.

2. AAT has acidcyalic,so after enabling of life time,acidcyalic has been separated and it happens in liver.

-It is anti-serinprotease enzymes.

Revenue:

-AAT is an

Including :

1. $\alpha_1$-antichymotrypsin

2. $\alpha_2$-antiplasmin

3. Antithrombin III

4. herparin cofactor II

5. $C_1$ inhibitor

6. ovalbumin

7. TBG

-After AMG, It is secondary proteinase inhibitor in plasma.

-Inhibitor for for most of the serin protease including :

1. Trypsin

2. calicyrine

3. Renine

4. ureakinase

5. plasmin

6. Thrombin

It connected to enzymes which have serin active site and makes them disabling.the most importance inhibitor of blood proteinases is $\alpha_2$–macro glubuline and the second one is AAT. The most importance inhibitoredserinportase is alastase.

-In phagocytosis time,Neutrophiles release some enzyme that names elastt(destroyes the alastine).which injuring the cells.Body for resistance to this damage produces one enzyme that names AAT.

-Alastine is in lung in breath and expiration causes to opening and closing of alleoles , in other words if there was not alastin,breath and expiration could not happens.

-amphysmiadesease creates because of ATT deficiency.

-torment respiratory new-born syndrome : (RTS)

-because of dificting , synthesis the surfactant(pheonomocytes-II)

-The most essential and most importance matter of it are sequentially lesitin and Dipalmitoieclecitine which hinders from both connection and obstruction of alleoles.

-for measuring of lesitin to sphyhgomyeline.

Pedigree uses from Aminiouticliquid.If this pedigree has been two or more than two,so the person has torment respiratory new-born syndrome.

-The persons which have autoimmune and chimiotropy,type II of phenomocyt wipes out so these persons have RTS.

Clinical importance of ATT :

Increasing:

-Acut phase Response

-Esterogen

*Decrease :

-Genetics deficiency       piss 60% ,pimz 6%

-Alcohol    pimm 100%,pizz 15% , piz 35%

-urea excretion and GI:Bothproxymale tube injuries and entrophathyNephrogenic syndrome loses protein.

-Increase of AAT using creates torment respiratory new-born syndrome (RTS).

Reference InteravalseAAT :0.9 to 2.0 g/l

4.Alpha2-macroglabulin (AMG):

-It is an inhibitor of proteinase.

-It has four same chains.

-It behaves like as an inhibitor in this waywhich prevents from connecting of protein to enzyme.

-It is the first protease of blood.

-The same chains connectes together in dimer shape with Non-covalence junctions.each one of monomers inhibits one enzyme and prevents from attaining of substra to enzyme.

Figure : Alpha2-Macroglobin

-AMG is an inhibitor of proteinase.

-Including four same chains.

-preventing by reaching of protein to enzyme.

Function :

-Inhibiting of enzymes of the pathways such as lynin,compleman,coagulation and fibrinolysis.

-Receptor and transfere of proteinases to serienes.

-Transfer of small peptides (cytokinines),growthfactores(Insuline and growth hormone),Bivalent kation(cation)(zinc)

Clinical importance:

Increase :estrogen,Nephrogenic syndrome

Decrease : Acute phase response,pancreatic and prostatic cancer.

Reference Intervals=1.3 to 3.0 g/l

-It is Negetive-APR.

5.Alpha 1- Fetoprotein(AFP):

-It is an glycoprotein with 70 kilodalton (KD) weigh and 4% carbohydrate.

-It is the main protein of feotus scram which the most amount of it has been observationed after three mounths of pregnancy.

-It synthesizes by liver and gall-bladder.

-It causes to connection and unactivation of esterogen.

-It is the substitute of Albumin.

*Estrogen increases in pregnancy priod in mother body which is dangerous for foetus so AFP connects to it and unactivated it.

-It is the receptor of Estroide hormones(ER, α,β) surface of membrane,nucleus and cytoplasm.

Clinical importance:

-Diagnosis of foetusdificies and chromosomal disorders.

-Increase :neural tube defect,ventral septum opening

-Decrease: Trisomy 21( down syndrome),Trisomy 18

-Marker of hepato cellular carcinoma and germ cell

Newborn ⟶ less than 5 mg/l

>180mo ⟶ less than 2 mg/l

6:Beta 2-microglobulin(BMG)

-It has low molecular weigh.(11.8 KD)

-The light chain (B-chain( is human lucocytal Antigen.

-It is single-strand and does not have carbohydrate.

-Its demi-consonant is 107 minates.

-It locates on all of body nucleollar cells surface.

By B-lymphocytes and tumoral cells releases in blood specially.

-human luokocytal antigen names HLA.

Clinical importance :

-It increases in renal failure, flaming and neoplasmy.

-It is the best of ranal tubules function.(specially in kidney transplantation.)

-It uses forcontinuoscalture of B-cells tumor.

-It increases in lucemia and lymphocytosis with CNS deficiency in CSF.

-In flaming,B-lymphocyte increases so AFP increases.

5.C-Reactive protein (CRP):

-connection to c-polysacharid Bactria septum.(cell wall)

-connection to cell wall polysaccharidies of Bacteries fungi and protozoan.

-connection to phosphorlycolyn, lesietin and polyaniounes(Neucleic acids) because of calcium absence.

-It synthesis in liver and is bare of carbohydrat.

-It increases because of infectious flaming.(But according to new resourses it increases in all of the flamings.)

-It reactesunespicial response to flaming and spicialy to infection.

-It causes to activation of classic compoleman pathway by starting of $C_{19}$.

-It performes phagocytosis by $C_{3b}$.

-It causes to opsonization.

-It causes to detoxification of autogenic compounds.

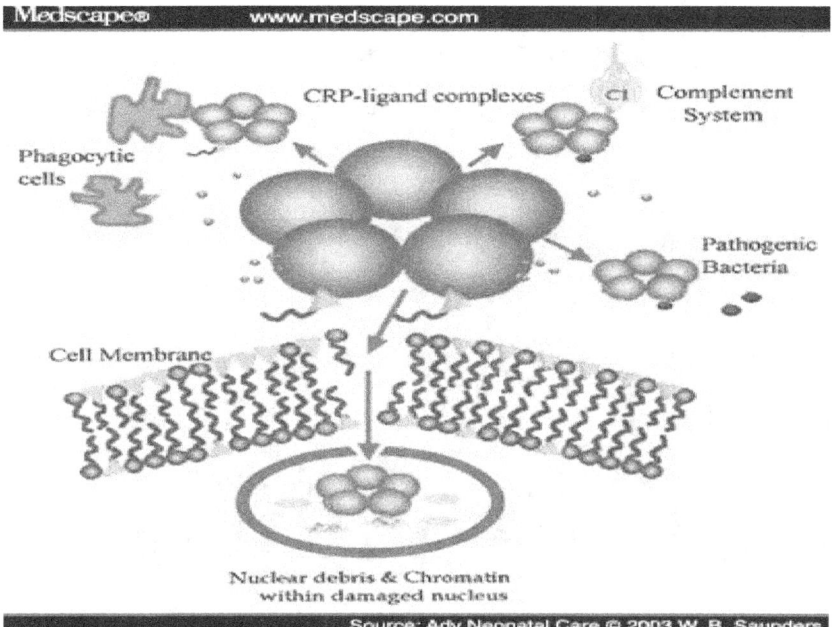

Figure 73: CRP-metabolism

-In Laboratory studies CRP by uglitination method.

# C-Reactive Protein

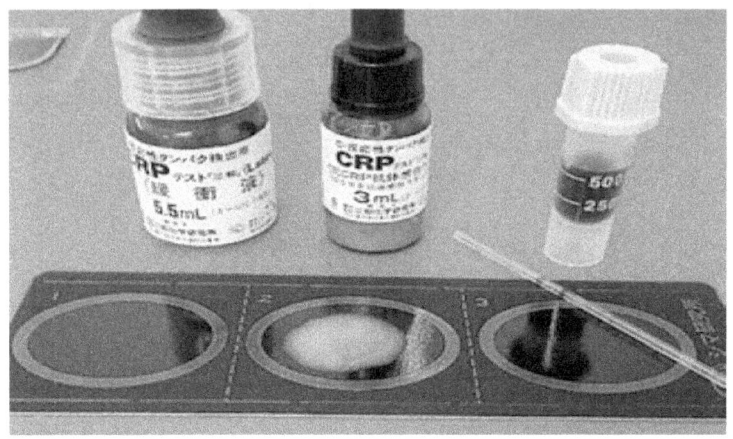

Reference Interval < 5 mg/L

Figure 74 : CRP

Reference Interval<5 mg/l

6.Retinal-Binding protein (RBP)

-It synthesis in liver and expelles by kidney.

Its transfer accomplishes as entirely trans retinol.

-It causes to majorized of glomerulus file teration.

-It causes to stability of Retinol-RBP complex.

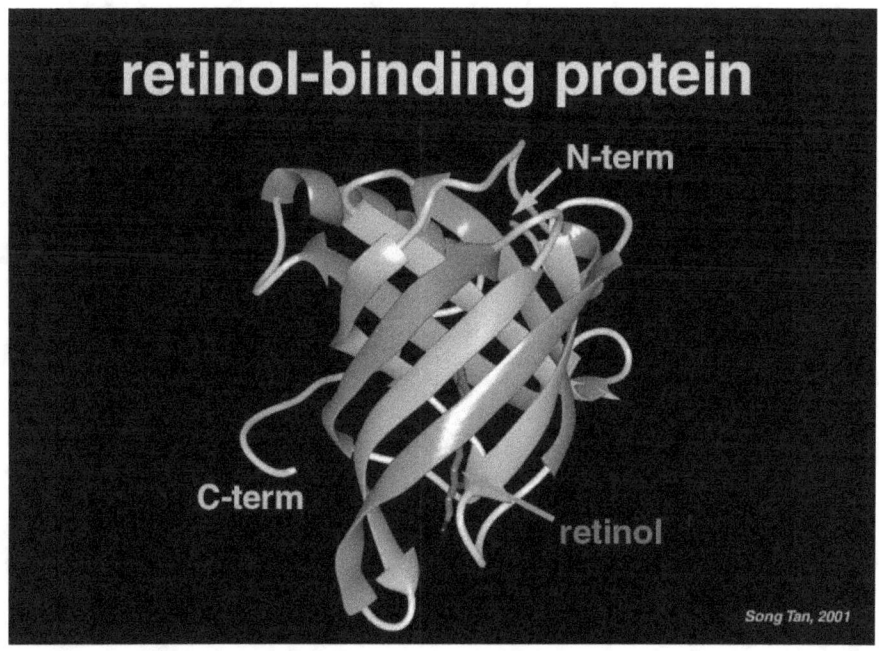

Figure 85 :Tridimentional RBP structure.

-ESR Rate increases in all of the non-infectious flaming

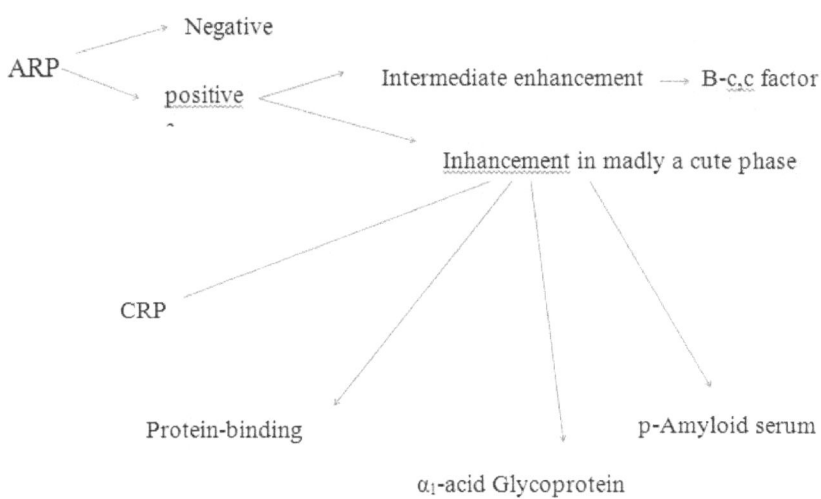

m-CRP increases 48-hours or 6-12 hours after flaming wheih the rate of this enhancer is two-thousand times.

m-CRPinhanceres in following occasiones :

-Stress

-Infection

-MI

-Thrombus

-In neoplastic reproduction (cancer)

-Spread brain cancer

Clinical importance :

Increase:

-proximal tubule injury

0Diabeties,Heavy metals

Decrease :

-APR

-Liver diseases

-malnutrition

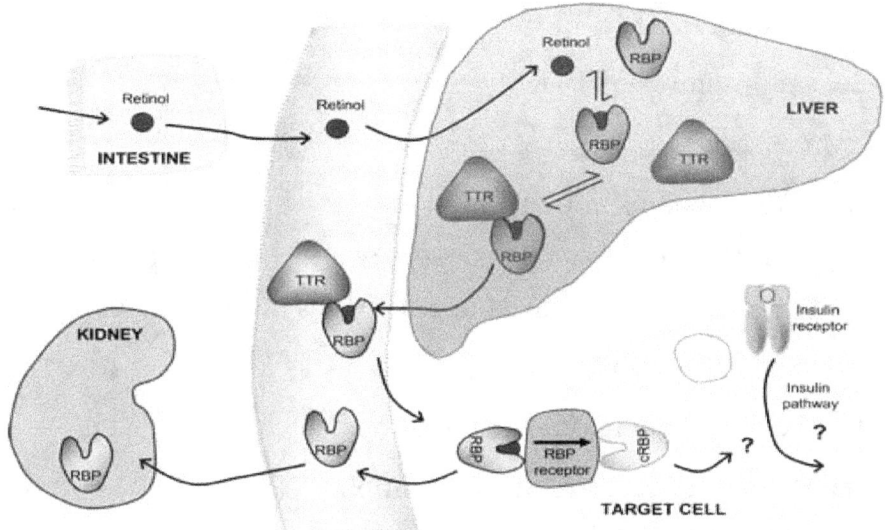

Figure 86 : RBP function

Per-Albumin is the band which its accasion is before Albumin and RBP Locates this band.

-RBP transfer,accomplishes as entirely trans Retinol,for transfer of Retinol needs to TTR (Because TTR causes to strength of Retinol and has transferred it to all the Locations.

-In malnutrition Both of RBP and TTR decreases.

-Retinol positive-RBP complex having a role in pathway of insulin action.

7.Pre-Albumin(Trans

-Transfer of $T_3$, $T_4$ (10%)

(10% of thyroid hormones transferes by par-Albumin and the remaining transferes by TBG).

Clinical importance :

-Generator tumors of TTR

-Liver deseases

-In hankered connection of $T_3$, $T_4$ (eutyroidhyperthyroxinemia)(Deseasewhitch are not related to gland of thyroid only connected protein has disorder.)

-Declined connection to $T_3$, $T_4$

-It is the third importance protein of body.

-The Rate of it decreases in malnutrition.

-It is the genetics variant of TTR.

8.Ceruloplasmin (Cp):

-It locates in $\alpha_2$–band

-It has 6-8 copper(blue color).

-Copper connects by an ATpase which there is not in wilson,s disease.

-Albumin and Trans copperyn,also,are the transfer of copper.

-It synthesis in liver.

-It is needed for folding of Cp.

-It is one of the most importance bands in $\alpha_2$.

Cu      ATpase    →   cp

            Causes to

-copper increases and subsides in the tissuse such as cornea,RBC,liver,brain.

In cornea $\longrightarrow$ creates brown loop around it.

In RBC $\longrightarrow$ creates Anemia

In liver $\longrightarrow$ creates cirrhosis.

In brain $\longrightarrow$ creates neural disorders.

-In absence of cu,ATpase,synthesis the cp but devastates instantly.

-The primary reason of cp is its gene decrease.

1.one of the secondary reason is copper decreasing in apportionment of nutritious.

2.Impermeable in reeasing of cu to GT.

3.Impermeable in intering of cu to ceruloplasmin but not causes of ATpase.

4.cu losing syndromes.

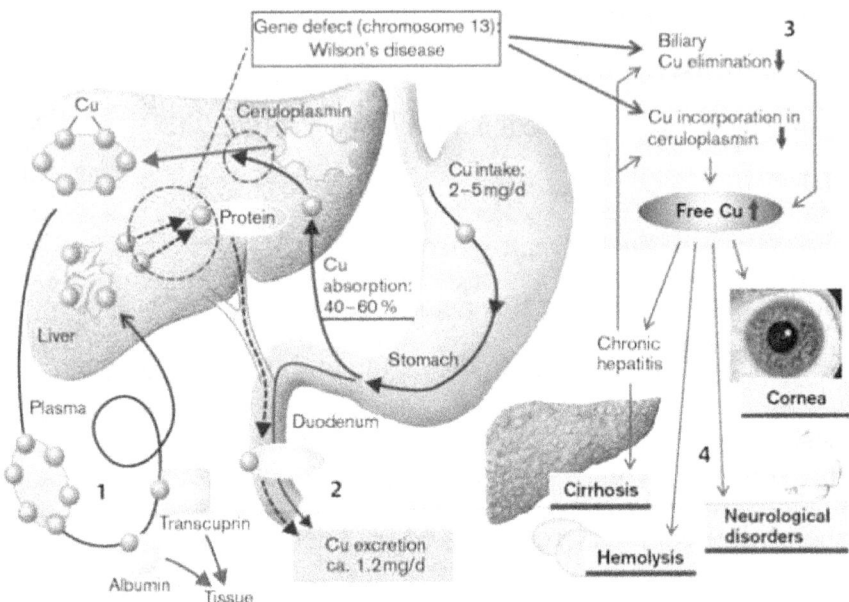

Figure 77: ceruloplasmin function in connection to copper

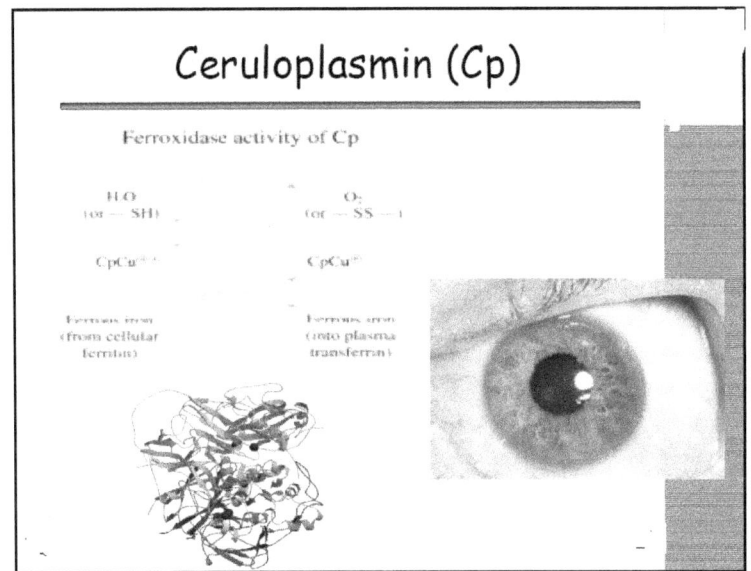

Figure 78 :ceruloplasmin mechanize

-Insuffinciency of copper creates Anemia.

-ceruloplasmin (fre-oxydase) causes to ferrous absorption.ceruloplasmin helps to transferring of fcrrity,s is bivalent and transperyn'sferruse is trivalent.

-The drug of Wilson's disease is penicillamine($C_5 H_{11} No_2 S$) which chelates ferrous.

-The drug of thalassemia's disease (ferrous insufficiency) isDesefrall(desfryoxamin).

9.Haptolobin (Hp):

-It synthesizes in liver and including two subunits which names α and β.

-It preventes of renal excretion of both ferrous and hem.

-Hp-Hb complex is an intense peroxidase.

-Hp is an bactericidal factor.

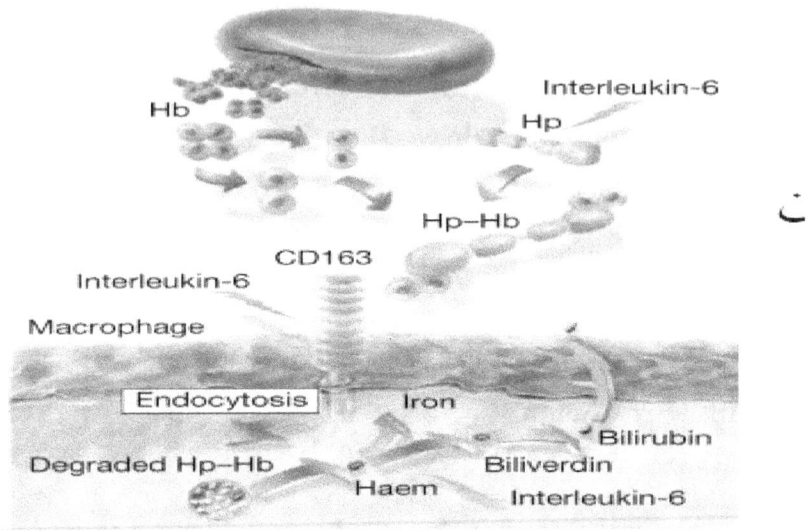

The Hp-Hb complex is engulfed by the macrophage and digested to release haem.
Dennis, C., Nature 2001 409(6817) p141-143

Figure 79 : Haptoglobin function mechanize.

-Hp (haptoglobin) connectes to hemoglobin.

-The accepted ferrous of some bacteries function obtaines from connected ferrous to Hp.

-In view of the fact that Hp is an bactericidal factor, Bacteriawipping out when ingestes the Hp-Hb complex.

Processes of Macrophages function :

1. connection of Hb to Hp.

2. Endocytosis into Macrophageswith interference of $I_6$

3. Disintegration (Decomposition)

Clinical importance:

-Increases by means of corticosteroids.

-It is the sensitive indicator of hemolysis;decreasing of Hphappenes via hemoglobinuria.

-Increase of estrogen causes to decreasing of Hp.

-Hp increases by corticosteroid.

*contray to others proteins of plasma,which had studed to this extent,each protein that increases by cortines,will be decreases via estrogen.

# Chapter 4

## Liver

Types of liver damage include:

- ❖ acute
- ❖ Chronic

- The main symptoms of liver disease that causes the application to be tested include:

Weakness, fatigue, anorexia, nausea, vomiting, abdominal swelling and pain, dark urine and light stools, and jaundice.

- Also, in patients with suspected viral hepatitis, family history of diabetes, liver disease, alcoholics, and in patients taking other hepatotoxic medications may cause an application to be tested.

**Acute liver damage**

- Call to an acute injury in short duration.
- The experimental proved: aminotransferase increased, which include:

(ALT=SGPT and AST=SGOT)

Increased to 8 times normal

- Often associated with increases in bilirubin.

Total Protein is not a measure of diagnostic accuracy: Due to an increase in immunoglobulin.

- Aminotransferase levels in acute damage include:

AST: 200 U/L

ALT: 300 U/L

- In some cases enzyme level increases up to 10 times as normal.

## روش اندازه‌گیری آمینوترانسفرازها

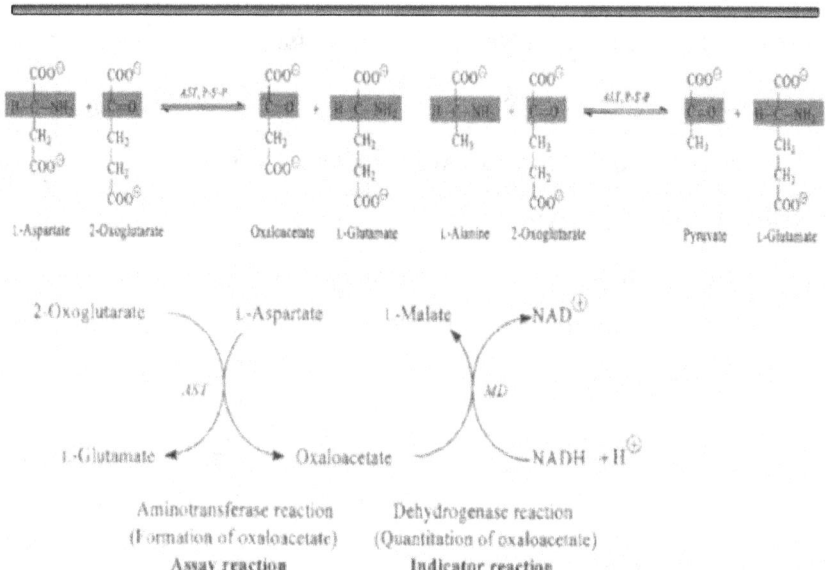

Table 90: Methods of measurement of aminotransferase.

## alkalen phosphatase (ALP)

- alkalen phosphatase found in the liver, bone, kidney, intestine and placenta of pregnant women.
- The maximum amount of this enzyme in the liver and bone.
- this enzyme found in bile ducts cell wall and produce in bone by osteoblasts.
- Increasing indicate liver and bone disease.

_Its degree increases so much in occlusion of hepatic tract.

_It increases fewer in liver cancer ,liver's injurious drugs,hepatitis and cirrhosis.

_The osteal isoenzyme of its increases as the formation of bone is increasing .for example in diseases like as pazhet disease and artherit romatoied.

_Rate of osteal isoenzyme is hiegh in physiological nature.

_Feeding cuases to partial increase in intestinal isoenzyme of ALP.

_Gamma-glutamyl transferase or 5-nucleotidase test is usefull for differential diagnosis osteal diseases from hepatic diseases.

_Both GGT and 5-nucleotidase just increases in hepatic diseases.

**REASONES OF LOW RATE OF ALP:**

_Blood transfusion,standing cardiac surgery,zinc insufficiency,an genetics bone rare disease names hypophosphatasia.

_The enzyme rate increases in pregnancy.

## SOME SPECIAL DRUGS CAUSEA TO CHANGE OF THIS ENZYME RATE:

_Antifertility pills causes to decrease of it and anticonvulsant drugs causes to increase of it.

## MEASURING OF ISOENZYMES BY MEANS OF TEMPERATURE:

Because of placental's isoenzyme resistant to heat(temperature),it is possible to located the sample in 65'c temperature for 30 minutes and measured the isoenzyme.

*Rigane's isoenzyme which increases in cancers also has the above characteristic.

_Hepatic's isoenzyme has most resistant to 56'c temperature rather than osteal's isoenzyme.

_Maximal rate of enzyme is for osteal isoenzyme;while after locating the serum in 56'c temperature for 10 minutes,less than 20 percentage of enzyme activity remains.

_Maximal activity is for osteal isoenzyme,if remainder activity was between 25-55%.

Measuring of isoenzymes by means of urea :

_Maximal resistant to urea is for both placental and intestinal isoenzymes.

_Hepatic isoenzyme has the average rate.

_Osteal isoenzyme has maximal sensivity.

_In acute hepatic damage ;jundice is an inconstant signal.

_In fants which are infectious to viridal hepatitis,jundice is rare and if happens,its rate is less than adults.

In adults,it has dependence to ethiology:

The rate of jundice is as following in adults:

*Hepatitis A→70%

*Hepatitis B→33-50%

*Hepatitis C→20-33%

*The rate of direct bilirubin to total is similar in both acute hepatic damage and biliary tract occlusion:

_Both are more than 50%.

_In 16% of patients is less than 50%,which in this situation must will had studied hemolysis.

Damage intensity testes in acute hepatic injuries:

_There is no connection between maximal rate of aminotransferases and complication's prescience.

_In some cases the decrease of enzyme activity accompanies by increase of damage intensity.

_The most indicator for recognition:PT test

_INR is more than 6.5.

_There is increase of death probability rate in this case.

_In viridal hepatitis;total protein rate is more than 15mg%.

_In alcoholic hepatitis;total bilirubin is more than 25mg% and albumin is less than 2.5mg%.

The main recognition for acute hepatic damages includes below cases:

- Viral hepatitis,alcohol,toxic and escymic reasons.

_If the rate of ALP be more than 2000 norm,first recognition is toxic and escemic damages.

_In poisoning by ACETAMONOPHEN ,rate of ALT increases to more than 3000 norm.

_These hight amounts is related to primary steps of damage (first hours 24)then decreases.

_Because the date of AST is less than ALT,there is most intensive decrease in acute hepatic damages.

If there isn't toxic reasons,the next studing case is viral hepatitis which is as follow:

IgM

Anti-HAV

HBsAg

Anti-HCV

HCV-RNA

If rate of aminotransferases be less than 300,but patient has clinical symptoms of hepatic damages,below cases must studies;

_Measuring the rate of AST to ALT.

_If be more than 2 and patient uses alcohol,so the result is alcoholic hepatitis.

There is uncommon reasons of hepatic damages in below cases:

Willson's syndrom

Autoimmune deseas

Hepatitis E

Other virouses

Acute hepatic damage:

It is common damage by mild and non-individualizid symptoms.

**Chronic liver injury**

- Common side effects of mild and nonspecific symptoms

- Diagnosis by biopsy and Study of liver

- Degrees of inflammation and fibrosis is seen that often along with fibrosis

- The risk of cirrhosis and liver cancer

**In the absence of biopsy**

- ALT continues for more than 6 months after acute hepatitis

- Unexplained increase in ALT more than once in the space of six months.

- Sometimes, despite being normal ALT, there is liver lesion.

- the Way to solve the problem is repeat testing over time.

- rejection of Chronic liver injury if it is 3 times the normal water.

- In people with normal ALT levels, they have chronic hepatitis in biopsy :

- Inflammation , fibrosis and cirrhosis are less likely to convert than those who

have high ALT.

- The most useful index for the assessment of chronic liver lesions , is ALT.

In all chronic liver lesions ALT level is higher than the AST;

With the exception of alcoholic hepatitis and timing of the cirrhosis;

- the level of (Bil D وBil t) and also ALP is natural.

Since Alt also exists in skeletal muscle, it needs intense exercise to increase body

and muscle effects to be considered.

- Measurement of creatine kinase helps in the diagnosis .

- In study of chronic liver injury , in addition to Serial of ALT should also

pay attention to the following points :

Primarily study consisted of physical examination, history of medicine, with emphasis on Taking the drug and laboratory kits for viral hepatitis.

- Evaluation of autoantibodies such as anti-nuclear or anti-smooth muscle antibodies, especially in young women or children for autoimmune hepatitis.

- Study ceruloplasmin for Wilson's disease in individuals under 40 years.

- Study of iron, transferrin, ferritin on suspicion of hemochromatosis.

- Evaluation of anti-mitochondrial antibodies and anti-neutrophil cytoplasmic Antibodies (ANCA) in chronic increase in ALT and GGT for the diagnosis of primary biliary cirrhosis and primary sclerosing cholangitis.

- Liver biopsy for inflammatory and fibrotic lesions of chronic And evaluate steatosis and alcoholic hepatitis diagnosis, especially in obese patients.

# Chapter 5

## Plasma lipids
**Lipids transfer in plasma**

-insolvent lipids in water transfered by plasma lipoproteins.

-special complexes containing special carrier proteins called apolipoproteins transfer lipids in plasma.

Different classes of plasma lipoproteins involve:

Chy, LDL, VLDL, HDL

Amounts of protein, phospholipid and density contain orderly:

HDL>LDL>VLDL>chy

Amounts of free cholesterol and estercholestrol contain orderly:

Chy>VLDL>LDL>HDL

Amount of triacilgliserol contains orderly:

Chy>VLDL>LDL>HDL

**Plasma lipoproteins**

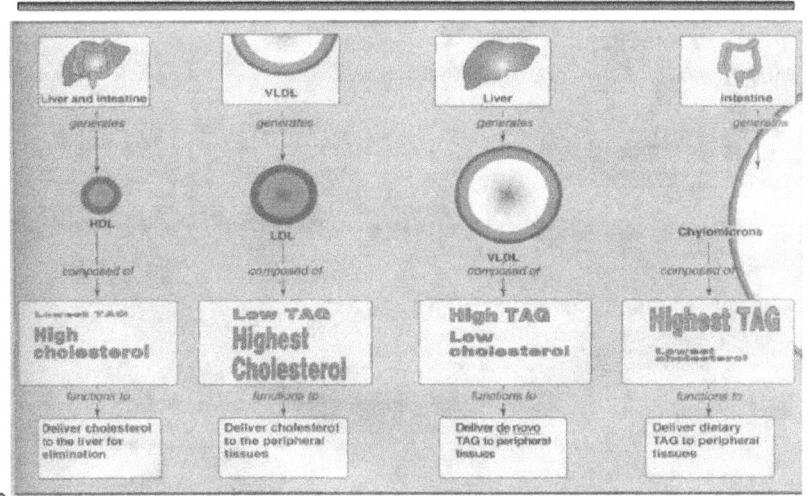

## Lipoproteins

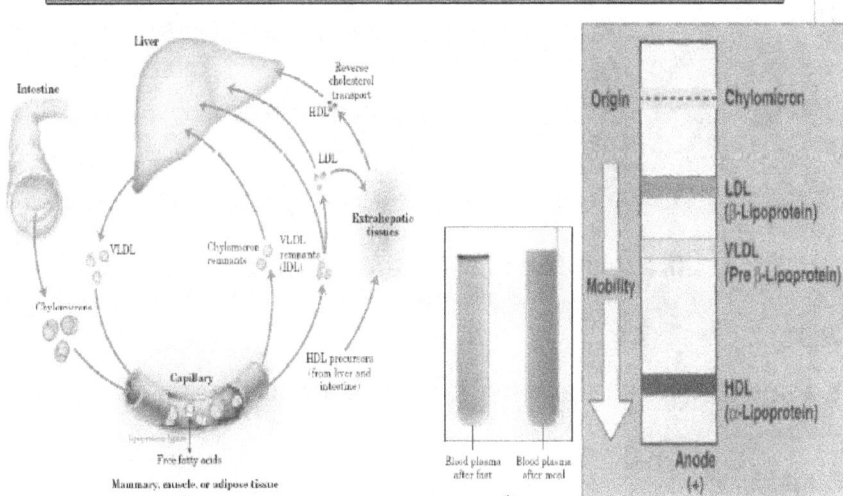

Figure91.plasma lipoproteins

| Apolipoprotein | Molecular Weight (Da) | Chromosomal Location | Function | Lipoprotein Carrier(s) |
|---|---|---|---|---|
| Apo A-I | 29,016 | 11 | Cofactor LCAT | Chylomicron, HDL |
| Apo A-II | 17,414 | 1 | Not known | HDL |
| Apo A-IV | 44,465 | 11 | Activates LCAT | Chylomicron, HDL |
| Apo B-100 | 512,723 | 2 | Secretion of triglyceride from liver binding protein to LDL receptor | VLDL, IDL, LDL |
| Apo B-48 | 240,800 | 2 | Secretion of triglyceride from intestine | Chylomicron |
| Apo C-I | 6630 | 19 | Activates LCAT | Chylomicron, VLDL, HDL |
| Apo C-II | 8900 | 19 | Cofactor LPL | Chylomicron, VLDL, HDL |
| Apo C-III | 8800 | 11 | Inhibits apo C-II activation of LPL | Chylomicron, VLDL, HDL |
| Apo E | 34,145 | 19 | Facilitates uptake of chylomicron remnant and IDL | Chylomicron, VLDL, HDL |
| Apo(a) | 187,000-662,000 | 6 | Unknown | Lp(a) |

Figure92.classification of human s plasma apolipoproteins

**Intra and extra-cellular estrification of cholesterol**

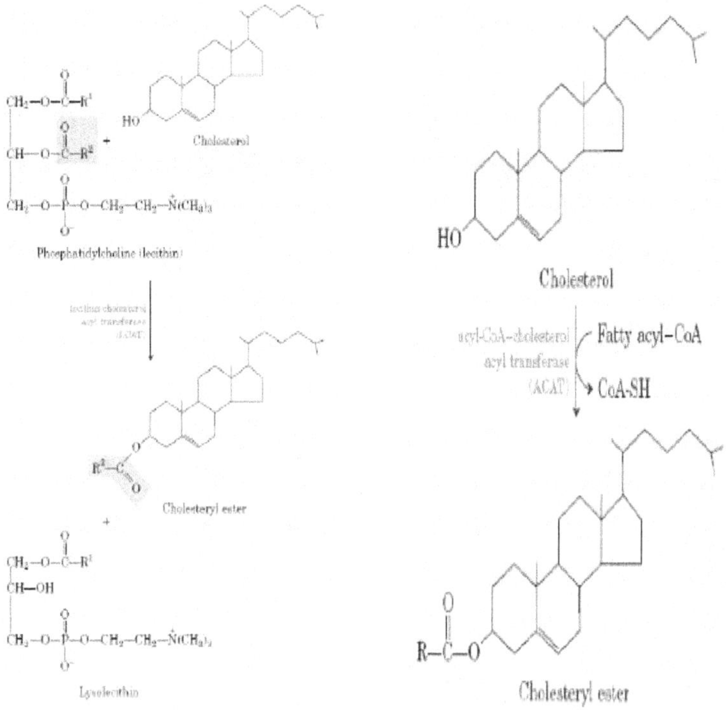

Figure93. intra and extra-cellular estrification of cholesterol

## Taking of cholesterol from depend-receptor endositose

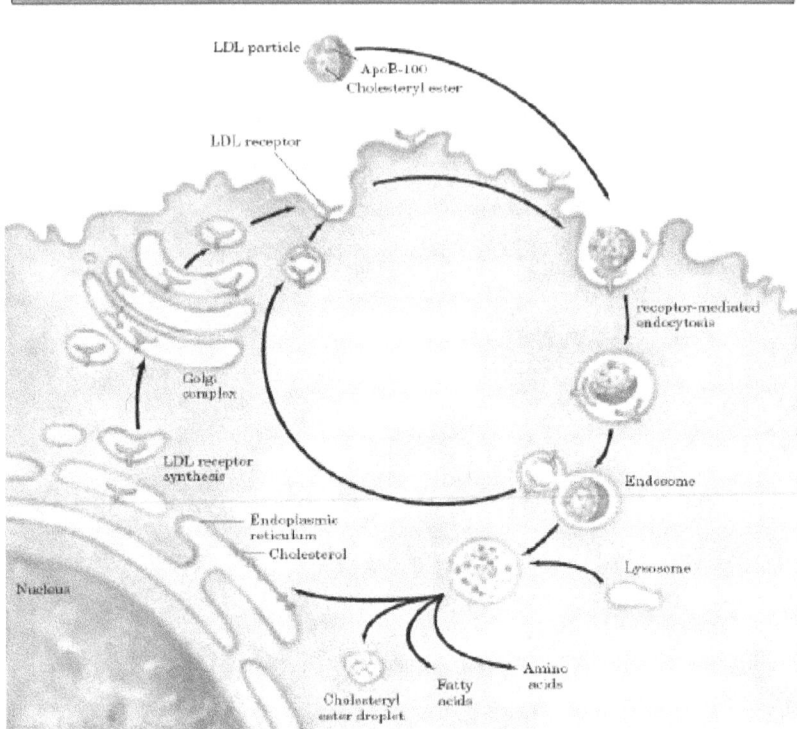

Figure94.taking of cholesterol from depend-receptor endositose


## Cholesterolester transferring protein(CETP)

-pure transferring of cholestrolesters and triglycerides among VLDL, LDL, HDL facilitated by CETP in blood circulation.

-this protein attaches to LDL in plasma.

## HDL metabolism

-HDL producd in liver and generated in lower levels in intestine.

-it acts as apoE and apoCll stocks.

**Reverse cholesterol transfer**

-replacement of additional cholesterol from cells and their transfer to liver for excluding cholesterol and biliary salts by HDL called reverse cholesterol transfer.

-free cholesterol transfer to HDL causes to nascent HDL production. this action done by ribbon carrier attached to(ABCA-1) ATP. Phospholipid transfer done by this carrier to nascent HDL causes HDL3 production.

-cholestrol ester transfer to HDL3 causes HDL2 production.

-HDL2 concentration in plasma is proportional to LPL activity.

-as the more LPL activity, the more HDL2 amount.

-LPL, liver lipase, LCAT, released by heparin(HRHL).

-rate of atrosclorosis has a reverse relationship with HDL2 amount.

- liver lipase and TG and phospholipids of HDL2 external layer causes cholesterol release and its absorption by liver and finally causes HDL3 production.

-endrogens (virile hormones) cause increase of liver lipase activity and estrogens(feminine hormones) cause decrease of this enzyme activity.

-HDL2 concentration in women s blood is more than men s blood.

## HDL metabolism

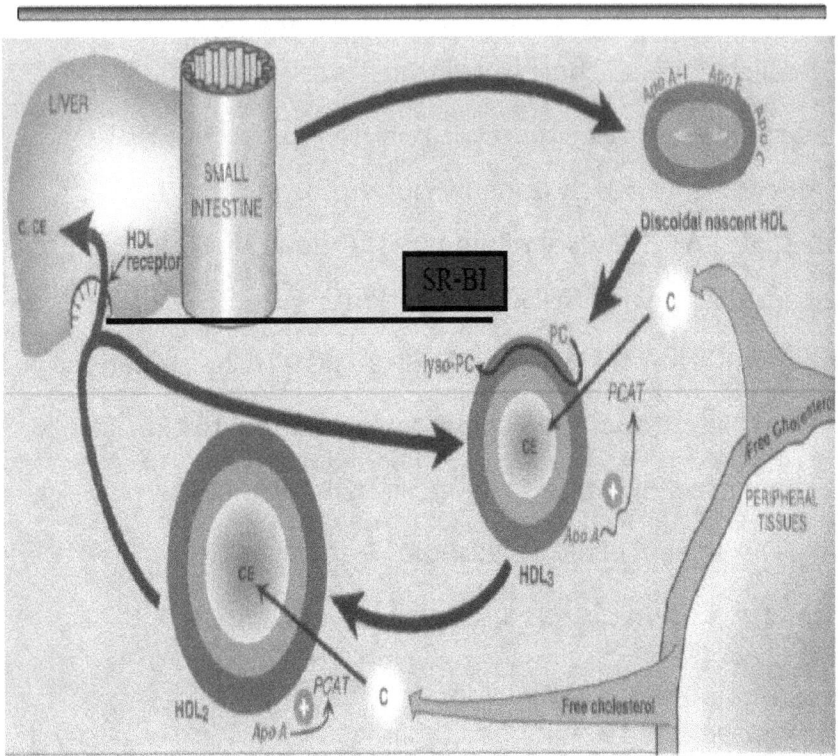

Figure95.HDL metabolism

## Cholesterol measurement

### .Liberman-borshard method

-cholestrol makes colorful compounds with solution of powerful acids.

- the color in circumference relates to cholestanid sulfanoic acid.
- both free and cholesterlester are measured in this reaction.

## Probable mechanism in LIEBERMAN-BURCHARD and ZAK reaction

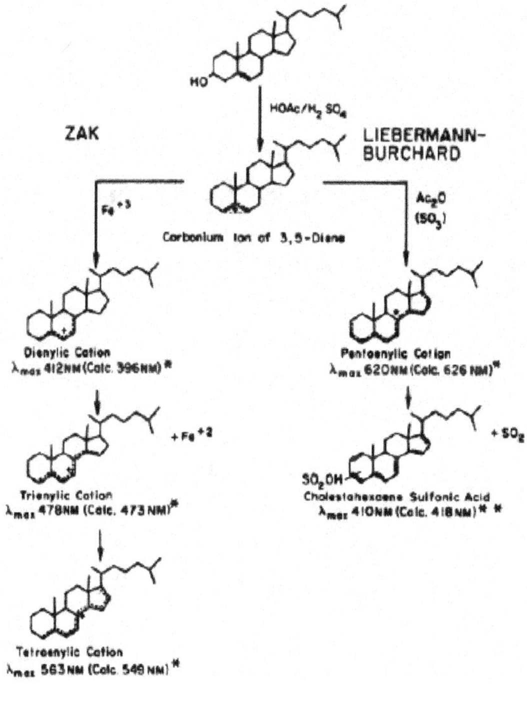

Figure96. proable mechanism LIEBERMAN-BURCHARD and ZAK reaction.

**Enzyme measurement method of cholesterol**

-in this method, cholesterol is measurable in 5-500 mg/dl range.

-ascorbic acid up to 5 mg/dl concentration, bilirubin up to 20 mg/dl concentration, hemoglobin up to 200 g/dl concentration and triglyceride up to 200 mg/dl cause none disorder in experiment.

-the samples which concentration above 500 mg/dl should be diluted by Physiological serum.

**Enzyme measurement method of cholestrol**

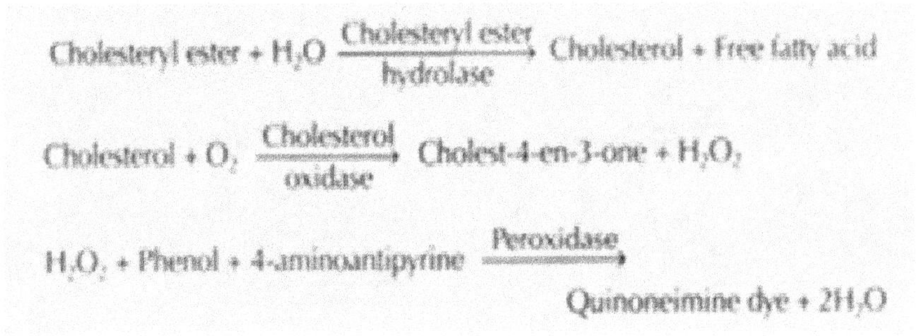

$$\text{Cholesteryl ester} + H_2O \xrightarrow{\text{Cholesteryl ester hydrolase}} \text{Cholesterol} + \text{Free fatty acid}$$

$$\text{Cholesterol} + O_2 \xrightarrow{\text{Cholesterol oxidase}} \text{Cholest-4-en-3-one} + H_2O_2$$

$$H_2O_2 + \text{Phenol} + \text{4-aminoantipyrine} \xrightarrow{\text{Peroxidase}} \text{Quinoneimine dye} + 2H_2O$$

Figure97.enzyme measurement method of cholesterol

**Triglyceride measurement**

-enzyme and chemical methods

-chemical method done by soaponification with potasium or transesterization with alkooxidaz

-glycerol releases from triglyceride structure and is oxidized to formaldehyde by sodium peridate.

-in next stage, formaldehyde compounds with solforic acid and produces a colorful solution.

-free glycerol in circumference is one of the most important sources that creates mistake in both chemical and enzyme method.

-don't use fresh serum.

-hydrolise of triglycerides done by lipase serum.

-up to 700 mg/dl is linear.

**Basis of triglyceride measurement in enzyme method**

$$Triglyceride + 3H_2O \xrightarrow{Lipase} Glycerol + Fatty\ acid$$

$$Glycerol + ATP \xrightarrow{Glycerokinase} Glycerophosphate + ADP$$

$$Glycerophosphate + O_2 \xrightarrow{Glycerophosphate\ oxidase} Dihydroxyacetone + H_2O_2$$

$$H_2O_2 + Phenol + 4\text{-}aminoantipyrine \xrightarrow{Peroxidase} Quinoneimine\ dye + 2H_2O$$

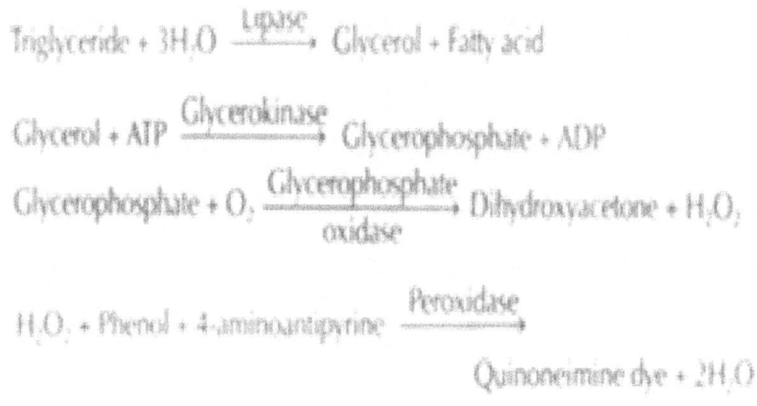

Figure98.basis of triglyceride measurement in enzyme method

## HDL-C MEASUREMENT

-source method:ultracentrifuge

-electrophortical method is the best method by accuracy and correctness about 20-40 mg/dl in clinic.

- most applicable method to separating HDL is using heparin - manganese.

## LDL-C measurement

-source metod ultracentrifuge

-electrophortical methods

-using freedval formula:LDL(mg/dl)=[tCh1]-[HDL+VLDL]

## Remedial panel of cholesterol

| | |
|---|---|
| **LDL cholesterol** | |
| < 100 | Optimal |
| 100-129 | Near optimal/above optimal |
| 130-159 | Borderline high |
| 160-189 | High |
| ≥ 190 | Very high |
| **Total cholesterol** | |
| < 200 | Desirable |
| 200-239 | Borderline high |
| ≥ 240 | High |
| **HDL cholesterol** | |
| < 40 | Low |
| ≥ 60 | High |
| **Triglycerides** | |
| < 150 | Normal |
| 150-199 | Borderline high |
| 200-499 | High |
| ≥ 500 | Very high |

Figure99.remedial panel of cholesterol

## Disorder of lipid metabolism

### Clinical signs of lipoproteins increase

1-lipid assembly in arterial: atromatose

2-lipid assembly in tissues of ender skin: xezantomatose

## Lipoprotein disorders

- Hypercholesterolemia
- Hypertriglyceridemia
- Mixed Hyperlipidemia

Hypercholesterolemia causes

Primary Hypercholesterolemia-

Familial Hypercholesterolemia Mvnvzhnyk which includes two modes:

- Homozygous: LDL receptor is absent
- heterozygous: LDL receptor-half normal.

Xantoma tendon and Xanthelasma was confirmed in early childhood is homozygous and heterozygous occurs only after the third decade of life.

Secondary hypercholesterolaemia caused by the following:

- Primary Hypothyroidism
- Dyabt Sugar
- Nephrotic Syndrome

- Klstaz
- Medications(Drug)

Mixed hyperlipidemia caused by increased production of apoB and is the result of LDL and VLDL.

## Hypertriglyceridemia

Primary hypertriglyceridemia, including:

- Increased blood Shylvmykrvn is due to LPL deficiency or deficiency of apoC.

Hypertriglyceridemia secondary

Mixed Hyperlipidemia

Endogenous familial hypertriglyceridemia due to:

- Obesity, glucose intolerance, decreased HDL, hyperuricemia

Mixed hyperlipidemia because:

- Increased cholesterol and triglycerides simultaneously
- Increased LDL and VLDL
- Aggregation LDL and Remains Shylvmykrvn
- ApoE deficiency: Type III(Broad beta band hyperlipidemia) or beta form Lypvprvtyynmya

Symptoms:

- Corneal curvature and Gzantlasma
- Tuberous Xantoma on knees and elbows

- Lipid deposits in the palmar incision
- High incidence of cardiovascular disease

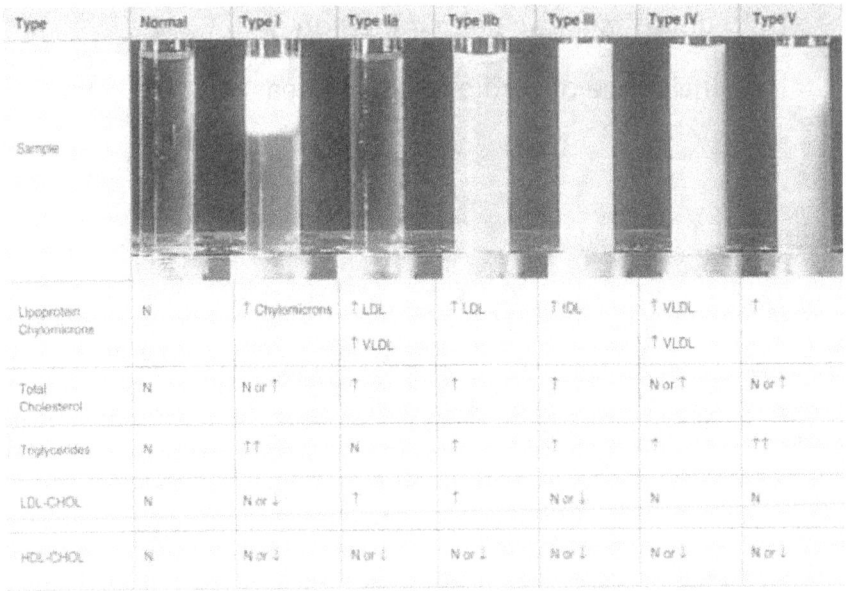

Figure100. classification of dislipidmya and its types

Eruptive xantoma that involves following symptoms:

-small, scratched and yellow nodule assembly

-increase of TGs concentration (VLDL and chylomicron)

-abdominal pains and acute pancreatic

-nodule would be destroyed by decreasing of TGs

-tuberous xantoma that involves following symptoms:

-yellow plaques in elbow and knee

-xanthelasma that is called as fat sediment in skin around eye.

-stock in tendons, Achilles tendon

-stock in cornea, in patient above 40 age

-IDL, chl, LDL

**Tuberous xantoma**

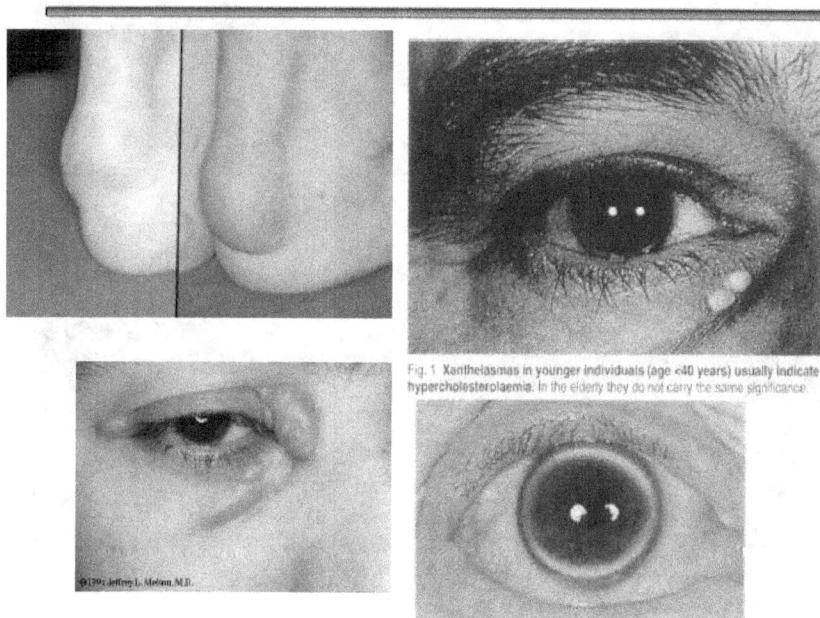

Figure101.tuberous xantoma

Plamar xantoma that involves the following symptoms:

-blood linear sediments of lipid in palm

-increase LDL

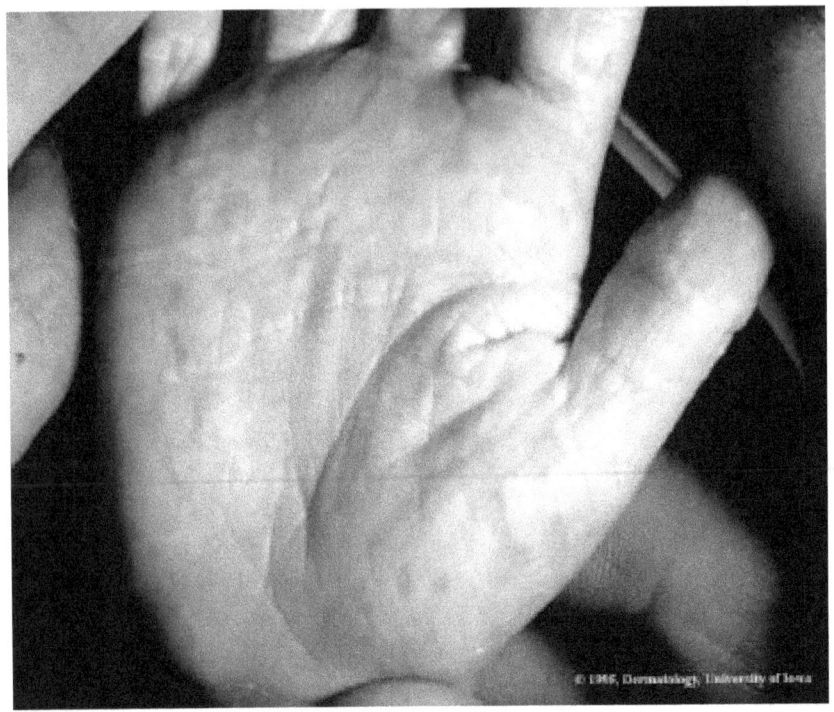

Figure102.plamar xantoma

# Refrences

Clinical biochemistry/hooshang amirrasooli-tehran:jafari 1387

Devlin biochemistry/javad zavarnia-tehran:khosravi-dibaj-1386

Harper biochemistry/reza mohammadi:tehran-aeizh-1386

www.ingramcontent.com/pod-product-compliance
Lightning Source LLC
Chambersburg PA
CBHW071352290426
44108CB00014B/1517